Sexual Shame in Women
and How to Experience Freedom

Sexual Shame in Women
and How to Experience Freedom

Joy Skarka

WIPF & STOCK • Eugene, Oregon

SEXUAL SHAME IN WOMEN AND HOW TO EXPERIENCE FREEDOM

Copyright © 2022 Joy Skarka. All rights reserved. Except for brief quotations in critical publications or reviews, no part of this book may be reproduced in any manner without prior written permission from the publisher. Write: Permissions, Wipf and Stock Publishers, 199 W. 8th Ave., Suite 3, Eugene, OR 97401.

Wipf & Stock
An Imprint of Wipf and Stock Publishers
199 W. 8th Ave., Suite 3
Eugene, OR 97401

www.wipfandstock.com

PAPERBACK ISBN: 978-1-6667-3646-5
HARDCOVER ISBN: 978-1-6667-9478-6
EBOOK ISBN: 978-1-6667-9479-3

APRIL 18, 2022 8:27 AM

All Scripture quotations, unless otherwise indicated, are taken from the Holy Bible, New International Version®, NIV®. Copyright ©1973, 1978, 1984, 2011 by Biblica, Inc.™ Used by permission of Zondervan. All rights reserved worldwide. www.zondervan.com. The "NIV" and "New International Version" are trademarks registered in the United States Patent and Trademark Office by Biblica, Inc.™

Thank you to those who supported me while I completed my dissertation. Thank you for your love, support, encouragement, and prayers:
my husband, Zachary Skarka
my parents, John and Debra Pedrow
my first reader, Dr. Sandra Glahn
my second reader, Dr. Sue Edwards
my mentor, Dr. Juli Slattery.

Contents

List of Illustrations | ix

Preface | xi

Chapter 1	Introduction | 1
Chapter 2	Previous Research and Literature Review | 16
Chapter 3	Procedure and Research Method | 55
Chapter 4	Research Findings | 62
Chapter 5	Conclusions and Implications for Further Study | 97

Appendix A	Qualitative Survey Questions | 113
Appendix B	Quantitative Survey Questions | 115
Appendix C	Francesca (Participant #21) | 120
Appendix D	Ashley (Participant #9) | 122
Appendix E	Brooklyn (Participant #16) | 124
Appendix F	Tanisha (Participant #34) | 127
Appendix G	Grace (Participant #28) | 130
Appendix H	Jessica (Participant #6) | 134
Appendix I	Wendy (Participant #26) | 137
Appendix J	Holly (Participant #37) | 140

Appendix K	Anna (Participant #22)	142
Appendix L	Andrea (Participant #20)	144
Appendix M	Bailey (Participant #29)	147
Appendix N	Adaobi (Participant #14)	149
Appendix O	Zendaya (Participant #27)	152
Appendix P	Jennifer (Participant #35)	154
Appendix Q	Aubrey (Participant #15)	157
Appendix R	Stacy (Participant #28)	160
Appendix S	Brandi (Participant #11)	163
Appendix T	Carrie (Participant #44)	165
Appendix U	Jackie (Participant #38)	167
Appendix V	Juliana (Participant #24)	169
Appendix W	Victoria (Participant #18)	171
Appendix X	Kayla (Participant #2)	174
Appendix Y	Megan (Participant #42)	176

Bibliography | 179

List of Illustrations

Figures

1. Age of Participants (Qualitative Survey) | 58
2. Age of Participants (Quantitative Survey) | 59
3. Participants' Sexual Issues (Qualitative Survey) | 66
4. How Free the Participants Feel (0–100) (Quantitative Survey) | 67
5. How Free the Participants Feel (0–100) Correlated with Ages (Quantitative Survey) | 67
6. Comparing Ages with Sexual Shame (Quantitative Survey) | 68
7. Sexual Shame Caused Participants to . . . (Quantitative Survey) | 70
8. What Sexual Acts Made/Make Participants Experience Sexual Shame (Quantitative Survey) | 72
9. What Social Factors Made/Make Participants Experience Sexual Shame (Quantitative Survey) | 75
10. Non-biblical Sources That Provide Freedom from Sexual Shame (Quantitative Survey) | 80
11. Biblical Sources or Spiritual Actions That Provide Freedom from Sexual Shame (Quantitative Survey) | 81

List of Illustrations

12. Sources That Provide Freedom from Sexual Shame (Qualitative Survey) | 84
13. Time Spent Studying the Bible Correlated to Freedom from Sexual Shame (Quantitative Survey) | 88
14. Church Attendance Correlated to Freedom from Sexual Shame (Quantitative Survey) | 90
15. Christian-Community Involvement Correlated to Freedom from Sexual Shame (Quantitative Survey) | 90

Tables

1. Spiritual Maturity (Quantitative Survey) | 60
2. Self-Worth (Quantitative Survey) | 61
3. Q4 and Q6 Correlations (Quantitative Survey) | 77
4. Q4 and Q7 Correlations (Quantitative Survey) | 78
5. Q4 and Q8 Correlations (Quantitative Survey) | 78
6. Age Correlations with How Participants Experience Freedom from Sexual Shame (Quantitative Survey) | 82

Preface

THIS RESEARCH PROJECT EXPLORES how Christian women have experienced sexual shame and how they have experienced freedom. Two surveys were created to explore the research question. The first survey was quantitative and was completed by 1,090 Christian women. Those who were thirty-one to forty years old made up the majority at 30.73 percent, followed by those who were twenty-three to thirty years old, who made up 30.46 percent. The second survey was qualitative and was completed by forty-four Christian women. Of this number, 38.64 percent were twenty-three to thirty years old.

Two surveys designed by the researcher gathered both quantitative and qualitative responses with both closed and open-ended questions. The qualitative survey allowed women's voices to be heard and their challenges to be known in regard to the sexual shame they have experienced. The quantitative survey provided statistics to prove that women struggle with sexual shame and to show how they have found healing. The surveys asked questions about the woman's life as a Christian, self-worth, and experience with sexual shame. These questions explored correlation of involvement in Christian activities with levels of freedom from shame. The questions also examined what experiences and factors caused women to experience sexual shame and what non-biblical sources and biblical sources led to freedom from sexual shame.

The results revealed that women have experienced sexual shame from sexual acts and other social factors. The sexual acts

Preface

most mentioned that caused sexual shame were the following: masturbation, non-intercourse-related sexual contact (e.g., fondling, oral sex), and sexual fantasies or lust. The other factors that most led to sexual shame included the following: poor body image, the participant's church's views on women, and condemnatory comments from family and friends.

Because of sexual shame, women frequently felt far from God, lived a secret life, avoided prayer, and doubted that God loved them. At the time of the quantitative survey, the 1,090 women surveyed felt an average of 61 percent free from sexual shame. The extrabiblical sources that brought them the most freedom included empathetic friendships, sharing struggles with other believers, and intimate connections to others. The biblical sources that provided the most freedom included reminding themself of God's love, understanding that their sins (including shameful sexual acts) are forgiven through Christ's death, knowing that they have salvation through faith in Christ, prayer, understanding that God created humans as sexual beings, acknowledgement of God's forgiveness for their sexual past, and a sense of belonging in community.

The survey results aligned with the three hypotheses to reveal that Christian women identified understanding the love and grace of God, being known in biblical community, and learning a biblical teaching of sexuality as three contributors to finding freedom from sexual shame.

Chapter 1

Introduction

Importance of This Study

IN A WORLD IN which a rising number of women are addicted to pornography, research points to sexual shame as one of the factors that keeps women in bondage.[1] For women to find freedom from unwanted sexual behaviors, they first need to find freedom from sexual shame. Biblical shame can be used in positive ways, but this study will focus on the negative aspects of shame. As one will learn from this research project, sexual shame begins from many different avenues but is continued as Christian women fail to understand a biblical view of sexuality. Generally, instead of being sexually discipled by the church, women are sexually discipled by North American culture. Popular views of sexuality do not align with Scripture. Music, books, social media, and movies all send the message that people can have sex with whomever they want, whenever they want (sometimes not even with consent), with zero consequences. When women experience consequences because of

---

1. In 2021, the number of women watching porn was about 35 percent worldwide on the largest porn site. This is a 5 percent increase from 2020. More women are watching porn each year. The same site shared that in 2021, the second most searched for type of porn for men and women was "romance" or "romantic," which is a type that caters to female audiences, and the most searched type for women was "lesbian." Lastly, from 2020 to 2021, the category "popular with women" grew 41 percent ("Pornhub's 2021 Year").

their sexual choices yet fail to understand biblical sexuality, they experience cognitive dissonance, which can result in sexual shame.

Women in particular receive erroneous messages while lacking a shame-free response from many churches. Most commonly, churches remain silent on sexuality or preach a "just don't do it" message, instead of teaching a theology of sex and pointing hurting women to the grace of God. Because many women lack a view of healthy sexuality, they fail to understand that sexuality outside of God's design will hurt their sexuality and spirituality. Instead of pursuing sexual integrity in community, they often turn to sexual sin and, as a result, experience sexual shame—creating a vicious cycle of sin and hopelessness. In this project, readers will explore the literature and research that asserts that one of the key psychological issues of sexual sin is sexual shame. Sexual shame destroys relationships with others and disconnects women from God. Such shame also causes people to hide, isolate, expect rejection, hate themselves, and/or remain in addictive cycles, never finding freedom.

To help women break free from sexual strongholds, ministers are wise to start with the issue of sexual shame rather than behavior modification, because "out of the heart comes fruit" (Luke 8:15). To discover how women have found freedom from sexual shame in the past and to equip churches to minister in these issues, two surveys were conducted to derive information about how Christian women have experienced sexual shame and how they have found freedom from such shame.

Definition of Terms

In order to converse about the topics in the research project, readers should agree on what they mean by terms. Here are three key terms essential to the conversation:

Introduction

Shame

Shame can best be defined by examining three different areas of impact: identity, emotions, and relationships. Starting with identity, Curt Thompson, psychiatrist and shame expert, explains shame as a sense of "there being something wrong with me" and feeling powerless to change one's condition or circumstances.[2] Psychologist and trauma specialist Diane Langberg shares Thompson's belief: "Shame is not just a feeling, though it is profoundly that. Shame is a sense of the self—the 'I am'—as defective, empty, worthless, and trashed."[3] Popular shame researcher Brené Brown defines shame as "an intensely painful feeling or experience of believing that we are flawed and therefore unworthy of love and belonging."[4] In her study on women and shame, participants described shame using terms including "devastating," "consuming," "excruciating," "filleted," "small," "separate from others," "rejected," "diminished," "trapped," "powerless," and "isolated."[5] From this study, Brown found that women experience the most shame from specific categories, including the following: "appearance and body image, sexuality, family, motherhood, parenting, professional identity and work, mental and physical health, aging, religion, speaking out, and surviving trauma."[6] Jay Stringer, a licensed mental health counselor, ordained minister, and speaker on the subject of unwanted sexual behavior, defined shame as "the most painful experience that something you have done or failed to do has made you unwanted or unworthy of belonging."[7]

Secondly, shame is defined through negative emotions. In another study, Brown states, "Shame often produces overwhelming and powerful feelings of confusion, fear, anger, judgment and/or

---

2. Thompson, *Soul of Shame*, 24.
3. Langberg, *Suffering*, 126.
4. Brown, "Shame Resilience Theory," 45.
5. Brown, "Shame Resilience Theory," 45.
6. Brown, "Shame Resilience Theory," 46.
7. Stringer, *Unwanted*, 143.

the need to escape or hide from the situation."[8] Counselor Heather Davis Nelson defines shame as "a fear of weakness, failure, or unworthiness being unveiled for all to see, or fear that at least one other person will notice that which we want to hide."[9] Nelson believes that "shame is that lingering sense that I have failed beyond rescue. That I have failed because I am a failure."[10] She argues that "shame commonly masquerades as embarrassment, or the nagging sense of 'not quite good enough.'"[11]

Lastly, shame hurts relationships. Karen McClintock, a pastor and psychologist specializing in human sexuality, explains that "shame is a theological and psychological emotion . . . a feeling of unworthiness in the sight of God or significant other."[12] The feeling of shame causes a deep disgust with oneself and one's body, creating a fear of vulnerability that destroys relationships. The distress from shame leads to isolation from oneself, others, and God.[13] Shame creates a fear of being known and a sense of being unworthy of love—specifically, the love of God and others. The fear of feeling defective creates expectations that one will be embarrassed, unaccepted, disgraced, powerless, cast out, or made to feel as if she does not measure up. Without feeling worthy of that love, people continue to live in isolation, keeping God and others at a distance. Thompson further explains, "[Shame] positions itself in such a way as to keep borders tightly closed and vulnerability at a minimum."[14]

For this study, it is important to understand the difference between shame and guilt.

---

8. Brown, *I Thought*, 27.
9. Nelson, *Unashamed*, 17.
10. Nelson, *Unashamed*, 26.
11. Nelson, *Unashamed*, 17.
12. McClintock, *Shame-Less Lives*, 14.
13. Thompson, *Soul of Shame*, 113.
14. Thompson, *Soul of Shame*, 157.

Introduction

Shame (as Opposed to Guilt)

Research has been conducted on the link between sexual behavior and guilt, but little research has focused on sexual behavior and shame. Shame differs from guilt and affects sexuality differently. Guilt focuses on behavior, while sexual shame focuses on a person's perceived lack of worth due to his or her sexual desires and activities.[15] Brown explains the difference between guilt and shame: "Shame is 'I am bad.' Guilt is 'I did something bad.'"[16] Guilt blames behavior. Shame blames identity. Guilt comes from making a mistake; but shame takes that guilt to a whole new level. Shame says, "I am the mistake." For example, a woman who looks at porn and feels shame would believe that she will never find freedom, because she feels "unworthy" or "dirty." In guilt, she would respond with confession and forgiveness, but if she experiences sexual shame, she responds with hiding, secrecy, and rejection.

Research has shown that shame is less adaptive than guilt and has a negative impact on the sense of self and self-worth.[17] Shame, generally speaking, produces more negative results than guilt.[18] For believers, guilt focuses on the behavior and draws believers to God and others as they seek forgiveness, while shame focuses on the self and pulls people away from God and others as they feel like something is wrong with themselves. Guilt can drive people to become more like Christ, while shame creates deep psychological and emotional pain. Believers can confess their sins, which frees them from the guilt that follows sin. The apostle John wrote of Christ, "If we confess our sins, he is faithful and just and will forgive us our sins and purify us from all unrighteousness" (1 John 1:9). After confessing their sins, believers can live free from guilt because of Jesus's death on the cross.

This research project will look specifically at shame surrounding sexuality and thus labeled "sexual shame." Despite the

---

15. Murray et al., "Spirituality," 222–34.
16. Brown, "Listening to Shame."
17. Dearing et al., "Distinguishing Shame from Guilt," 1401.
18. Carboneau, "Religiosity," 7.

vast amount of research on shame, little research has been conducted specifically about sexual shame.

Sexual Shame

Sexual shame is a specific type or subcategory of shame. Patrick Carnes, a leading expert on sexual addiction, defines someone with sexual shame as "feeling profoundly ashamed for having sexual feelings and believing that a person is bad for having such feelings."[19] Sexual shame results in negative effects on psychological, emotional, and social well-being.

McClintock defines sexual shame as "a feeling of unworthiness in the sight of God or significant other due to a sexual thought, desire, behavior, experience, or abuse."[20] She believes that sexual shame should be considered a defeating illness, because it damages self-respect, intimate relationships, and relationships in communities of faith because of the intense level of feeling unworthy of connection. Out of all forms of shame, McClintock believes, "No other form of shame feels so private or drives us so deeply into hiding," and thus, "sexual shame is the most pervasive and emotionally devastating."[21]

Sexual shame hinders one's ability to give and receive love and often keeps people in a vicious cycle of sexual sin, isolation, and a sense of unworthiness. Marnie Ferree, MA, LMFT, CSAT, and a leader in the field of sexual addiction, believes that women who continue in addictive sexual behaviors continue to feel shame as they find themselves in the same situation of powerlessness over and over. As women continue in addictive cycles, they are ashamed of themselves, which confirms the original negative core beliefs.[22]

---

19. Carnes, *Don't Call It Love*, 306. For Sarah E. Kyle's similar definition, see Kyle, "Sexual Shame," 16. One study defined sexual shame as believing that one is perceived by others as sexually deviant or unlike the norm. See Volk et al., "Religiosity," 244–59.
20. McClintock, *Shame-Less Lives*, 132.
21. McClintock, *Shame-Less Lives*, 131–32.
22. Ferree, *Making Advances*, 37.

Introduction

Anne Stirling Hastings, LCP, PhD, who treats sexual shame, believes that "as long as shame is attached to sexuality, then sexual activity or awareness of oneself as a sexual person will bring unpleasant feelings."[23] These "unpleasant feelings" are sexual shame. Sexual shame may look different in each individual. To help find healing from sexual shame, one can look at where it first began.

How Sexual Shame Began

To better understand sexual shame, readers can start by looking in Genesis at the story of the fall, when sexual shame first enters the world. In the garden of Eden, God created man and woman. God saw all that he had made, and he said that it was very good (Gen 1:31). Man and woman fully knew and loved each other. They walked around naked and felt no shame. They took pleasure in one another. God blessed them and commanded them to be fruitful and increase in number (v. 28). Before the fall, in the words of Christopher West, man and woman "saw God's plan of love (theology) inscribed in their naked bodies and *that's exactly what they desired*—to love as God loves in and through their bodies. And there is no fear (shame) in love [1 John 4:18]."[24] Man and woman had no doubts, no fears, no shame, and their experience represented full acceptance of the human body. But when sin entered the story, the man and the woman experienced fear (shame) for the first time as they lacked trust for one another and hid. The fear or shame that surrounded their nakedness caused them to experience sexual shame for the first time. The original shame ("I am naked") is fear ("I was afraid").[25]

Pope John Paul II taught that "fear is always part of the very essence of shame."[26] He further explained the connection: "Genesis 3:6 speaks explicitly about the birth of shame in connection

---

23. Hastings, *Treating Sexual Shame*, 25.
24. West, *Theology of the Body*, 27.
25. Paul, *Man and Woman*, 244.
26. Paul, *Man and Woman*, 239.

with sin. That shame is, as it were, the first source of the manifestation in man[kind] . . . of what 'does not come from the Father, but from the world.'"[27] God did not desire for sexual shame to be a part of this world, yet sexual shame entered the story and caused man and woman to cover themselves so that the other person would no longer see their nakedness. They experienced sexual shame; they hid from each other. West expounds on Pope John Paul II's words: "This is why 'nakedness without shame' is the key for understanding God's plan for our lives—it reveals the original truth of love. God created sexual desire 'in the beginning' to be the very power to love as he loves."[28] The problem is that man and woman lived naked and unashamed for only a short time. Shame touches the first humans at the "deepest level and seems to shake the very foundations of their existence."[29] Sexual shame occurred when they experienced fear in their nakedness and vulnerability.[30]

The narrator of Genesis describes what happened next: "Then the man and his wife heard the sound of the Lord God as he was walking in the garden in the cool of the day, and they hid from the Lord God among the trees of the garden. But the Lord God called to the man, 'Where are you?' He answered, 'I heard you in the garden, and I was afraid because I was naked; so I hid'" (Gen 3:8–10). Shame causes humans to alienate from the love of God, which is the source of the fullness that God has created for mankind.[31] God responds to them by essentially saying, "I want to see you," and they respond with, "I was afraid because I could be seen, so I hid. I do not want you to see me."[32] Shame makes them hide from God, but God wants to see them.

Shame might have started in the garden of Eden, but it continues to influence people today. One factor in the prevalence of sexual shame today is a lack of education and conversations

27. Paul, *Man and Woman*, 238.
28. West, *Theology of the Body*, 27.
29. Paul, *Man and Woman*, 238.
30. Paul, *Man and Woman*, 173–74.
31. Paul, *Man and Woman*, 239–40.
32. Langberg, *Suffering*, 125.

Introduction

around sexuality. When churches remain silent about sexuality from a biblical perspective, the media's messages become the teachers, reinforcing and growing the divide between spirituality and sexuality. This divide allows for shame to grow.[33] McClintock noticed that people are more likely to leave the church between high school and young adulthood, stating, "Perhaps we have failed to notice that these years coincide with the peak years of people's sexual activity."[34] People will either experience one of the following ways to learn about sexuality: silence approach, education approach, or Sexual Discipleship.[35] The silence and education approaches should be defined to explain the better solution to sexual shame, Sexual Discipleship.

Definition of Approaches

Silence Approach

The silence approach refers to an approach in which sexuality is never talked about in the home, school, or church. In her research, Sellers explains that at least 80 percent of her clients (men and women in therapy for sexual shame) raised in the United States grew up in homes that were silent or spoke negatively about sexuality and sexual development.[36] Sellers explains the problem in the following way: "When kids do not feel safe asking questions about their body and pleasure, and when they don't feel safe exhibiting normal curiosities about their genitals and pleasure, they learn shame."[37] Parents fear or feel awkward having conversations about sex, but research has shown that if a child feels offense or shame toward genitals and sexuality, such feelings can have a lifelong

---

33. McClintock, *Sexual Shame*, 12.

34. McClintock, *Sexual Shame*, 12.

35. Slattery, *Rethinking Sexuality*, 9–18. Sexual Discipleship is a trademark by Dr. Juli Slattery with Authentic Intimacy. Read more about the approach and ministry at https://sexualdiscipleship.com.

36. Sellers, *Sex*, 6, 105.

37. Sellers, *Sex*, 105.

negative effect on sexual pleasure and even sexual function.[38] Refraining from having discussions about sex and/or unintentionally divorcing God from sexuality is not a solution.[39] Children need to hear sex talked about in a God-honoring, beautiful way that helps them transition from childhood to adulthood. Failing to do so may lead a child to associate sex with silence and shame.[40]

Parents and church leaders may use another method, the education method, to teach that pleasure is bad and sex is dirty. But both approaches create fear and sexual shame.[41]

Education Approach

The education approach stems from a desire to educate someone about sex in order to prevent sexual behavior. While there can be some good in the education approach, it tends to be a one-time conversation rather than the creation of a more globalized discipleship model. The education approach often fails to present the bigger picture of why God cares about sex. Instead, the education approach tends to focus on negative messages of what to avoid instead of the positive message of beauty in God's design for sexuality.[42] For example, one therapist explained that all of her Christian clients expressed that sexual desire was wrong or impure. She believed this view of desire was because the only messages preached at her clients' churches about sexuality involved education about what to avoid doing with the opposite sex.[43] If a child hears only "Sex is bad. Just don't do it," that child may experience sexual shame as his or her body develops and begins to desire sex. Another negative parental reaction might include responding poorly to a daughter getting her first menstruation or needing a

38. Rough, *Beyond Birds and Bees*, 79.
39. Hastings, *Treating Sexual Shame*, 26.
40. Stringer, *Unwanted*, 38.
41. Chapin, *Facing the Talk*, 168.
42. Stringer, *Unwanted*, 62.
43. Sellers, *Sex*, 4.

Introduction

bra—resulting in the daughter's sexual shame.[44] Imagine such a young girl experiencing sexual shame at home over her period, and then getting "the talk" at church, during which she is told to cover up her body because it could "tempt" the boys. When a young woman gets the "modesty talk" and a young man gets the "porn talk," leaders often set the stage for the young woman to experience sexual shame. The "modesty talk" creates shame for the young woman, as she may believe that her body causes her peers to turn to pornography.

The education approach tends to focus on preventing "bad" things from happening. There is a difference between avoiding consequences of sex and stating that desire is wrong. To clarify, it is a good thing to save sex for marriage so that sex is consensual and free of shame. However, usually when religious communities practice the education approach, the message focuses on eradicating desire, which results in sexual shame.[45]

Research shows that the education approach does not present a positive view of sexuality but rather creates more shame. For example, research presented by Christine Watkins in *Do Abstinence Programs Work?*[46] reveals that "messages contained in abstinence-only-until-marriage programs typically rely on fear and shame-based messages to convince young people to remain abstinent."[47] Other research, presented by Calah Alexander in *Do Abstinence Programs Work?*, validates the conclusion that abstinence-only education paints a picture that sex before marriage will make people "dirty and worthless."[48] Yet, while God does desire for his children to abstain from sex before marriage, he does not want his children entering marriage full of sexual shame and fear. The abstinence-only approach removes characteristics of a loving and forgiving God. Those who have endured such teaching tell horror stories of unmarried girls who had sex being compared to chewed-up pieces

---

44. Hastings, *Treating Sexual Shame*, 17.
45. Stringer, *Unwanted*, 62.
46. Watkins, *Abstinence Programs*.
47. The Healthy Colorado Youth Alliance, "Raising Expectations," para. 14.
48. Alexander, "Sloppy Seconds Sex Ed," para. 10.

Sexual Shame in Women and How to Experience Freeedom

of gum, an Oreo cookie chewed up and spit out, cups of spit, and plucked roses, which instill feelings of worthlessness and shame that can continue even after marriage.[49] Alexander explains that such an approach to sex education "doesn't teach children what sex is, what their sexuality means, how to understand it, or how to properly integrate it into a life of chastity both without and within marriage."[50] Instead, such teachings bring sexual shame both to those who have sexually sinned and to those who "wait" until their wedding night.[51] While the article was not written from a Christian perspective, the findings it describes are still true for Christian woman who hear negative messages in church.

Another aspect of the education approach is the message that one is promised a great sex life in marriage if he or she abstains from having premarital sex. This message sets people up to distrust God. When people are promised a happy and fulfilling sex life in marriage if they abstain from having sex beforehand, people can suffer disappointment when sex is difficult or challenging. God is viewed as a liar who cannot be trusted. The same phenomenon often happens when people are promised a marriage partner in a message from a church leader, but they are still single—they think God failed to keep his word. And such a disappointment also creates sexual shame as a result of believing something is wrong with them (shame) and/or something is wrong with God (affects faith).

Both the silence approach and the educational approach were a part of the purity-culture movement (further addressed in chapter 2), which has led to many women experiencing sexual shame. Sexual shame is passed on from generation to generation through the way sex is talked or not talked about. The stories told or not told in homes, communities, and churches can determine if a woman may experience sexual shame.[52] The silence approach and the education approach both differ from a third approach: Sexual Discipleship.

49. Alexander, "Sloppy Seconds Sex Ed," paras. 8–9, 11.
50. Alexander, "Sloppy Seconds Sex Ed," para. 10.
51. Alexander, "Sloppy Seconds Sex Ed," para. 11.
52. Thompson, *Soul of Shame*, 92.

Introduction

Sexual Discipleship

Sexual Discipleship must be clearly defined, because it is one possible proposed solution to the sexual-shame problem. Unlike the education model, which usually has a time frame, the discipleship approach is for a lifetime. Dr. Juli Slattery, cofounder of the ministry Authentic Intimacy, states the purpose of Sexual Discipleship: "Instead of telling you what to think, it trains you how to think."[53] Christian leaders can help people learn how to think about sexual issues by creating safe, grace-filled environments in which people can ask questions, explore sexual desires, and learn how to integrate sexuality and spirituality.[54] Failing to integrate one's spirituality and one's sexuality can cause people to live fragmented lives that operate at two contradictory levels: disembodied spirituality and suppressed bodily sexuality, which often results in unwanted sexual behavior.[55] Instead of separating sexuality and spirituality, Sexual Discipleship combines the two. Sexual desire is a good, God-given desire. Integrating this concept is foundational for people as they learn about sexuality, how to channel it, manage it, and appreciate it.[56]

Research Question and Expected Results

This study asked and answered the question "How do women experience sexual shame and how have they found freedom?" The following hypotheses were formed prior to the research process:

1. Christian women will identify understanding the love and grace of God as a key factor in finding freedom from sexual shame.

---

53. Slattery, *Rethinking Sexuality*, 21. Learn more about Authentic Intimacy's passion to reclaim God's design for sexuality at https://www.authenticintimacy.com.
54. Sellers, *Sex*, 14.
55. Hirsch, *Redeeming Sex*, 42.
56. Sellers, *Sex*, 14.

2. Christian women will identify being known in biblical community as a key factor in finding freedom from sexual shame.
3. Christian women will identify learning a biblical teaching of sexuality through Sexual Discipleship as a key factor in finding freedom from sexual shame.

Research Design of the Study

Christian women were anonymously surveyed through qualitative and quantitative surveys. In the qualitative survey, these women were asked open-ended questions so the researcher could collect stories and learn how women have found freedom (survey attached at the end in Appendix A). In the quantitative survey, they were asked questions using the Likert scale and multiple-choice questions to collect data (survey attached at the end in Appendix B).

Limitations

Possible limitations include the following: not having enough survey responses, not having a diverse-enough representation of participants, not reading more secular resources on sexual shame, and not being able to get the survey into the hands of women unconnected to social media.

Other limitations include not asking correct questions in the survey or participants misunderstanding the survey questions. Upon reflection, it does not make sense for the quantitative-survey participant to pick "every day" for how often they attend church or for being in a Christian community where biblical topics are discussed, unless that participant serves in Christian vocation. Another possible limitation is not defining sexual shame for the survey participants. Lastly, one limitation could be from dishonest answers in the surveys.

Introduction

Preview of Remaining Chapters

Chapter 2 describes a research and literature review addressing sexual shame. The literature review addresses two specific contexts in which women experience sexual shame: (1) pornography and sexual addiction and (2) sexual abuse and assault victims. The chapter will then look at the research and literature of sexual shame specific to women and to Christian women. After seeing the vast problem of sexual shame, readers will explore the research and literature on how women have found freedom from sexual shame and unhelpful ways to remove sexual shame. This section concludes with the research and literature that closely aligns with the three hypotheses.

Chapter 3 presents the procedure and research method. In this chapter, the research questions and hypotheses are presented in light of the research subjects. The procedure and research method includes details of the process to design the instrument, the correlation process of the survey questions, the procedures, and the process of analyzing data.

Chapter 4 explains the research findings. The responses from the survey questions are broken down into the following categories: how women experienced sexual shame, how women experienced freedom from sexual shame, and the relationship to the three hypotheses. This chapter also shows all the correlations related to the hypotheses.

Chapter 5 summarizes and concludes the research by presenting research implications. This chapter includes the researcher's interpretation of results, implications for future ministry, and suggestions for future research.

In the appendix sections, readers can look at the qualitative survey, the quantitative survey, and the qualitative-survey results cited in the paper.

Chapter 2

Previous Research and Literature Review

Introduction

CHAPTER 2 INTRODUCES WHAT the literature says about sexual shame: (1) why sexual shame is a problem, with specific focus on sexual shame in pornography and sexual addiction as well as in sexual assault and abuse; (2) how sexual shame produces specific symptoms in women; (3) how sexual shame uniquely affects Christian woman; and (4) how women find freedom from sexual shame. Understanding how women experience sexual shame will equip ministers to know how to help women find freedom. In addition, this review of pertinent literature has informed the development of the two survey instruments used in the research project (Appendixes A and B).

Sexual Shame: The Problem

When people experience shame, they are likely to respond by fleeing and freezing.[1] Flee and freeze are the two responses that most specifically correlate with sexual shame. People will flee to sexual acts to numb the pain of sexual shame caused by the trauma. And freezing, as Langberg explains, "is dissociative—paralysis,

---

1. Langberg, *Suffering*, 136.

passivity—it is as if no one is home because if no one is home, then there can be no shame."[2] Of the two, freezing may be the more dangerous. But both fleeing and freezing demonstrate that sexual shame causes emotional, spiritual, social, and physical damage to women.

The next section will detail the issues regarding sexual shame and its influence on North American culture by looking at two specific issues: (1) pornography and sex addiction and (2) sexual abuse and assault. These two issues were chosen for in-depth research because they were common among the women interviewed in this research project.

Sexual Shame: Pornography and Sex Addiction

Carnes, an expert in sexual addiction, describes the relationship between sexual addiction and sexual shame: "Acting out relieves the tension, pain, and deprivation that pervade all parts of the addict's life."[3] And such acting out provides the person with a sense of immediate pleasure, relief, and numbness; however, the feelings disappear and are replaced with sexual shame. Carnes explains, "The addict feels like a failure. Once out of control, the addict scrambles to regain control. This 'acting in' becomes even more intense because the feelings of failure reinforce the preexisting feelings of shame."[4] An addict may reduce sexual shame to get out of repetitive cycles of unwanted sexual behaviors.[5]

Research has shown that sexual shame keeps people stuck in a cycle of sin and addiction.[6] Shame creates a feeling of powerlessness and the contributing factor in the belief that one is unable to stop addictive behaviors such as pornography.[7] The shame caused

2. Langberg, *Suffering*, 136.
3. Carnes, *Don't Call It Love*, 104–5.
4. Carnes, *Don't Call It Love*, 104–5.
5. Carnes, *Don't Call It Love*, 227.
6. Prosek et al., "Experiencing Shame," 126–38.
7. Carboneau, "Religiosity," 3. See also Struthers, *Wired for Intimacy*, 55–58.

from viewing pornography is a factor that triggers hopelessness. For example, individuals with a high level of shame combined with pornography addiction may feel hopeless to change and as a result, continue to use pornography for temporary relief from the negative feeling of shame.[8] The sexual addiction mixed with added sexual shame creates an increase in self-deprecating thoughts and feelings.[9] Repeatedly failing at attempts to find freedom from addiction leads to shame. Psychiatrist and theologian Gerald May believes that "in a passive response to defeat, the addicted person is besieged with feelings of shame, remorse, and guilt. The self-hatred may lead to suicidal impulses, but more often the person simply surrenders to the addiction."[10] Another study proved a similar point by stating that after someone experienced a sexual deviance or perceived a sexual experience as a misbehavior, sexual shame results as extreme emotional distress.[11] For example, when Christian young adults view watching pornography as a shame-based activity, they feel more sexual shame and, as a result, alienate themselves from God and struggle asking for forgiveness, which causes emotional distress.

Researchers argue about whether shame leads to addiction or addiction leads to shame. Carnes states that "shame emerges from addiction. Shame causes addiction. Whichever way the shame is flowing, whether consequence or cause, it rests on one key personal assumption: Somehow I am not measuring up."[12] Other researchers have concluded that shame is the force that drives the addictive system and behaviors.[13] Still another study has shown that in regard to pornography use, sexual shame is not a predictor of pornography use but a result and a method of dealing with

---

8. Chisholm and Gall, "X-Rated Addiction," 269; Rhea and Issler, "Identity Status," 155–67.

9. Chisholm and Gall, "X-Rated Addiction," 259.

10. May, *Addiction and Grace*, 47.

11. Murray et al., "Spirituality," 222–34.

12. Carnes, *Don't Call It Love*, 91.

13. Adams and Robinson, "Shame Reduction," 23–44.

shame.[14] Thompson agrees: "We continually look at pornography in no small part as a coping mechanism for our inadequacy that long precedes it."[15]

Those who experience greater shame are more susceptible to sexual addiction, including pornography addiction or other hypersexual compulsive behaviors.[16] Either way, if shame births addiction or addiction births shame, most clinicians agree that the process of shame reduction is crucial to the recovery process of sex addiction.[17] If shame remains unaddressed, sexual shame will most likely prevent healing and recovery for the sex addict. Other research supports the hypothesis that the only way to treat sexual addiction is to reduce shame.[18] Shame keeps women feeling overwhelmed, turning back to their addictive cycle, and back to compulsive behaviors to cope with the negative emotions. The only way out of the pornography addiction is to figure out what keeps one stuck in it. For many women, that factor is sexual shame.

One's involvement in religion also affects shame and sex addiction. Research found that those who are religious and morally disapprove of pornography experienced direct sexual shame when they looked at pornography.[19] A different but similar study also found that "the more one felt disconnected, or alienated from God, the more shame and guilt they also experienced."[20] This study concluded that those who felt alienated from God had a 47 percent increase in shame.[21] Another study looked at 186 people who had used pornography within the past six months and found that religiosity was a significant predictor of sexual shame, but not sexual

---

14. Gilliland et al., "Shame and Guilt," 12–29.
15. Thompson, *Soul of Shame*, 130.
16. Gilliland et al., "Shame and Guilt," 12–29; Dhuffar and Griffiths, "Role of Shame," 231–37.
17. Wilson, "Shame Reduction," 230.
18. Adams and Robinson, "Shame Reduction," 23–44.
19. Volk et al., "Religiosity," 244–59.
20. Murray et al., "Spirituality," 227.
21. Murray et al., "Spirituality," 231.

permissiveness.[22] Thus, sexual shame causes isolation spiritually, relationally, emotionally, and physically and is intricately connected to feeling spiritually alienated.

Because of the shame surrounding sexual addictions, especially for women, fear can prohibit healing. Former addict and now expert Ferree explains how fear inhibits healing: "The fear of being discovered in sexual sin makes it especially difficult for strugglers to ask for help. And when the problem has escalated beyond 'just' a rare or occasional sexual slip into the realm of sexual addiction, the shame can be paralyzing."[23] For people experiencing sexual addiction, sexual shame can be the glue keeping them stuck in the cycle of addiction.[24]

Sexual Shame: Sexual Abuse and Assault Victims

Women who experience sexual shame are often sexual abuse victims. Research shows that women with extensive histories of child abuse develop feelings of shame and blame themselves for the abuse.[25] This phenomenon may help to explain why women with sexual trauma have greater psychological symptoms, specifically shame, in adulthood.[26] In fact, one study showed that women who experienced childhood sexual abuse showed higher levels of shame and lower levels of self-esteem.[27] Bessel van der Kolk, psychiatrist and industry leader in studying and treating trauma, explains one reason victims of child abuse experience such shame: "Most of them suffer from agonizing shame about the actions they took to survive and maintain a connection with the person who abused them."[28] The sexual shame increases when the

22. Garcia, "Pornography Use," 66.
23. Ferree, *No Stones*, 29–30.
24. Birchard, *Compulsive Sexual Behaviour*, 177.
25. Arata, "Coping with Rape," 62–78; Feiring et al., "Trying to Understand," 26–41.
26. Briere et al., "Accumulated Childhood Trauma," 223–26.
27. Kemish, "Psychological Distress."
28. Van der Kolk, *Body Keeps the Score*, 13.

victims experience sexual pleasure during the sexual abuse. Dan Allender, PhD, a prominent Christian therapist, author, professor, and speaker focusing on sexual abuse and trauma recovery, is a victim of sexual abuse and felt pleasure during the sexual abuse. He describes what happened to him and what is common to other victims: "Our greatest shame is in responding to the touch of our body with arousal and pleasure. It is the darkest work of evil to mar our sexuality through the experience of touch. My body felt arousal through all my senses, and therefore sensuality is dangerous and dark."[29] As was true for Allender, any slight pleasure felt during sexual abuse causes a woman to experience sexual shame.

Sexual shame negatively affects the lives of victims, specifically causing them to think they are the problem, rather than the perpetrator. For teens, feeling shame can be traumatic in itself and can harm the adolescents' physical, psychological, social, emotional, moral, and religious development, and can negatively reshape their views of themselves and interpersonal relationships.[30] Statistically, girls who have been sexually abused as children mature sexually on average a year and a half earlier than the non-abused girls, because the sexual abuse speeds up their biological clocks and the secretion of sex hormones.[31] Then, the onset of early sexual desires and curiosities creates more sexual shame.

Women who experienced sexual assault as adults also experience sexual shame. In a study of women raped in adulthood who also experienced domestic violence by long-term partners, one interviewee said that she feels sexual shame about her sexuality and blames herself for the abuse.[32] Another woman wrote that she experiences sexual shame that keeps her in silence and avoiding her emotions.[33] The fear of speaking out and telling their stories brings more shame. Mary DeMuth, an author and minister helping

---

29. Allender, *Healing the Wounded Heart*, 42.
30. Denton, "Utilising Forgiveness," 5–28.
31. Van der Kolk, *Body Keeps the Score*, 165.
32. Reavey and Gough, "Dis/Locating Blame," 329.
33. Reavey and Gough, "Dis/Locating Blame," 337.

sexually abused women, states, "Shame flourishes in silence."[34] By "silence," she means both the silence the victim keeps by not speaking out and silence as a reaction from others. For women who come forward in their churches with sexual abuse and are met with silence, the lack of response creates more sexual shame. DeMuth says that often, "the first response by leaders in authority is denial, then survivor shaming and blaming."[35] Sadly, these responses in addition to the abuse itself can lead to depressive symptoms, post-traumatic stress disorder, and suicidal ideation.[36] People who have experienced any form of sexual assault or abuse are often plagued with sexual shame. While both men and women can experience shame from abuse, the research described below will demonstrate how this specifically affects women.

Female-Specific Response to Sexual Shame

Women experience sexual shame differently from men, yet most of the research surrounding sexual shame is about men.[37] Because women are different from men, women need separate research. This research project looks specifically at women.

Women experience different, and possibly far greater, sexual shame than men because women deal with specific negatives associated with sex: unwanted pregnancies and legal issues such as prostitution.[38] Women experience sexual shame when they deal

---

34. DeMuth, *We Too*, 41.
35. DeMuth, *We Too*, 126.
36. Alix et al., "Self-Blame," 1–16.
37. One study looked at a twelve-step program and added shame-reduction techniques for sexually addicted men. Researchers found that by reducing shame, twelve-step programs could reduce one's struggle with sexual addiction. The researcher describes the role of sexual shame in sexual addiction, arguing that "the cycle of addiction can be stopped by reducing shame through the transformation of shame-based core beliefs" (Griffin, "Shame Reduction," 6). One could argue that reducing shame-based beliefs in order to find freedom from sexual shame is true for women as well, but the shame-based core beliefs may look different.
38. Hottenstein, "Role of Shame," 7; Ferree, *No Stones*, 30–31; Dhuffar and

Previous Research and Literature Review

with sexual disorders such as vaginismus. Vaginismus is defined as "a condition in which vaginal spasms occur and prevent penetration during sexual intercourse."[39] Research has found that more than 32 percent of women have experienced some form of pain during sexual intercourse in their marriages, over 22 percent from vaginismus or other female sexual dysfunctions.[40] For those with vaginismus, 6.8 percent of the women experienced such intense pain that penetration with their husband was impossible.[41] One study observed pregnant women with vaginismus and found that they were less likely to follow up with their medical team after pregnancy due to feelings of shame from the medical staff failing to understand their vaginismus.[42] Many women experience shame because of physical conditions that are not necessarily related to sexual abuse, such as vaginismus—this is an example of body shame.

Carnes describes body shame as "a deep embarrassment about one's body or about certain aspects of one's body. People who feel body shame tend to continually compare themselves with others."[43] Both men and women may struggle with body shame, but they may struggle differently. Another definition of body shame is "the emotional response resulting from comparing one's body to a cultural or internalized standard and perceiving oneself as not meeting that standard."[44] As an example, most advertising portrays the ideal woman as impossibly thin, creating an

---

Griffiths, "Role of Shame," 231–37.

39. Achour et al., "Vaginismus and Pregnancy," 137.

40. Gregoire et al., *Great Sex Rescue*, 56. Although some have called into question the data in this resource, I've seen enough evidence in my own work to suggest that Gregoire's conclusions have merit apart from the controversy surrounding her.

41. Gregoire et al., *Great Sex Rescue*, 57.

42. Gregoire et al., *Great Sex Rescue*, 137–43.

43. Carnes, *Don't Call It Love*, 307.

44. Gervais and Davidson, "Objectification among College Women," 84.

Sexual Shame in Women and How to Experience Freeedom

unachievable standard.⁴⁵ Body shame could be a subcategory of sexual shame, since all bodies are sexual.

Historically, one can see how women's body shame has been affected throughout the centuries. For example, mothers often stopped talking to their daughters about their periods to protect their daughters' virtues. In the twentieth century, intimate maternal conversations with daughters were most often about the use of a particular product rather than about sexuality or reproduction.⁴⁶ At the turn of the twentieth century, young white women began to talk about their own sexuality. Their new language of sex was generated by North America's first great sexual revolution.⁴⁷ Studies of female sexual behavior in the early 1950s reveal that 41 percent of women who had premarital intercourse did so in a car.⁴⁸

Today, more than 50 percent of young women have intercourse, voluntarily or under pressure, before completing high school.⁴⁹ Girls' bodies are eroticized in the West at an increasingly early age.⁵⁰ Cultural messages create body shame for women every day, from the exaggerations in porn to the photoshopped billboards. The sex displayed on the screen is nothing like sex in real life. The performers are negatively affected by these influences, too. People acting in porn are usually high or drunk to be able to get through filming porn scenes all day; 79 percent of porn performers have used marijuana and 50 percent have used ecstasy.⁵¹ It is normal for the women in porn to be high, drunk, and have eating disorders, yet when other women watch porn, they see only the externals. Thus, women think about how their own bodies fail to measure up—resulting in body shame. Women believe they need to compete with the eroticized images of women, a phenomenon Ferree witnesses in her clients. She states, "Eroticized images of

45. Gervais and Davidson, "Objectification among College Women," 84.
46. Brumberg, *Body Project*, 40.
47. Brumberg, *Body Project*, 153.
48. Brumberg, *Body Project*, 154.
49. Brumberg, *Body Project*, 191.
50. Brumberg, *Body Project*, 191.
51. Griffith et al., "Pornography Actresses," 1–12.

women, sex, and love are so institutionalized they seem real, and women often find themselves competing with these internalized images of femininity."[52]

Carnes explains the impact of the unspoken standard combined with the stigma of being a woman with a sexual addiction: "They [women] add to their shame when they feel they must be the 'only' woman who acts this way—and it is that sense of uniqueness which is central to the secret world of any addict. Their loneliness represents the special burdens our culture places on women."[53] Loneliness keeps a woman stuck in the cycle of sexual shame.

Women also internalize the message that "to be worthy of love, a woman must be 'good.' But if she is sexual, she is 'bad.' So how can a sexual woman be a good person?"[54] This sense of "badness" quickly turns into an identity issue for women. Ferree explains this in the context of her own experience:

> The female sex addict quickly embraces an identity of shame, rather than seeing herself as created in the image of God. She questions whether God even loves her at all. How could she be a Christian and remain involved in sexual sin? The only way to make sense of that dual reality is to condemn herself. My own self-description (privately, at least) was "slut." I knew what I was doing was wrong; I knew I couldn't stop. The only conclusion must be that I was a horrible, terrible person.[55]

Perry's findings are consistent with those of Carnes and Ferree, but he blames the cycle of sexual shame on a lack of education of biblical sexuality, specifically equating sex and gender through stereotypes. Many Christian women are taught that porn is a male problem. Perry explains that Christian women wrestle in a unique way with a sexual shame that is unique to them because of "gender" stereotypes, because "they are forced to deal with the social challenges and intrapersonal turmoil of sinning against their

---

52. Ferree, *Making Advances*, 55.
53. Carnes, *Out of the Shadows*, 163.
54. Ferree, *Making Advances*, 55.
55. Ferree, *No Stones*, 30–31.

gender—sinning 'like a man.'"[56] This "double shame," Perry believes, is due to complementarian ideals of femininity, masculinity, sexuality, and gender stereotypes.[57] Thus, conservative Protestant women's porn use is particularly isolating, primarily because porn use is generally considered a man's sin. When women struggle with porn, they are referred to as "sluts." As a result, women tend to feel as if they need to hide their sexual sin more than men do.[58] Yet, sadly, women under age twenty-five are three times as likely as women twenty-five and older to seek out porn at least once a month.[59] And participation is not limited to single women. In a study of more than twenty thousand women who were married or have been married, eighteen thousand of whom were Christians, 13 percent reported using pornography and 3.7 percent reported binging on it regularly.[60]

Women could also be more likely to experience greater sexual shame than men possibly because historically, sexual sin has been viewed as more acceptable for men than women.[61] According to a study comparing men and women and shame, "Individuals who are female, younger, and with greater levels of femininity have higher shame scores."[62] Because women have more sexual shame, according to Ferree, women are more likely than men to remain silent.[63] People also believe that "the ultimate moral failure is admitting to out-of-control sexual behavior, and this is why most addicts remain silent."[64] Such dynamics are cultural and perpetuated by rape culture—a term that describes the normalization and frequency of sexual assault, violence, and victimization.[65]

56. Perry, *Addicted to Lust*, 90.
57. Perry, *Addicted to Lust*, 90, 105.
58. Schaumburg, *False Intimacy*, 156.
59. McDowell, *Porn Phenomenon*, 58.
60. Gregoire et al., *Great Sex Rescue*, 102.
61. Fugère et al., "Sexual Attitudes," 169–82.
62. Hottenstein, "Role of Shame," 26.
63. Ferree, "Females and Sex Addiction," 287–300.
64. Neill, "Problematic Sexual Beliefs," 67.
65. Skarka, "Forced Sexuality," 274.

Rape culture is filled with rape myths and victim blaming, which includes messages such as "She asked for it because of what she was wearing" and "Boys will be boys." Such messages propagate stereotypes about men as objectifiers and women as objects.[66]

One study looked at 489 young adult college women who were sexually objectified, and the research revealed that being objectified was directly related to depression because of shame surrounding "sexual objectification on body surveillance."[67] The study showed that to help women with depression, one had to help them lessen constant body monitoring, blaming themselves for being sexually objectified, and feelings of sexual shame.[68] These messages and the increase in rape occurrences have resulted in an increase in feelings of shame, self-blame, humiliation, and fear of public scrutiny—keeping women stuck in silence.[69] Unlike virtually any other crime, "when rape or sexual assault occurs, it is often the victims rather than the offenders who are blamed, humiliated, or defamed."[70] Rape culture allows men's sinful behaviors to be viewed as macho.[71]

While sexual shame is different for men and women, it is also different for Christian women and women who do not identify as Christian.

Sexual Shame Specific to Christian Women

When church leaders communicate specific messages about sex and gender that are unbiblical, people experience sexual shame. Both men and women are negatively affected by the lies; however, this section will focus specifically on the sexual shame Christian women experience. Carnes calls this "gender shame" and defines

---

66. Skarka, "Forced Sexuality," 274–79.
67. Szymanski, "Sexual Objectification," 135.
68. Szymanski, "Sexual Objectification," 135.
69. Weiss, "Too Ashamed to Report," 292–99.
70. Weiss, "Too Ashamed to Report," 289.
71. Schaumburg, *False Intimacy*, 156.

it as "a profound embarrassment and feeling of vulnerability about one's own sex, especially in relation to the opposite sex."[72] The previous section explored research about women in the general population experiencing more sexual shame than men, and additional research has suggested that such is also the case for Christian women.[73] One study found that in religious populations, sexual expression was often paired with shame and guilt, which resulted in classifying normal sexual development as altering the brain wiring.[74] As an example, Stringer told of how only women were instructed to refrain from premarital sex: "They were told not only to refrain from premarital sex but also to bury and run away from all sexual desire at the peak of puberty."[75]

Another example of poor biblical teaching on gender occurs in conversations about marriage. When wives are told the Bible commands them to submit to their husbands' sex desires so that the men's eyes will not look at another woman or at pornography, these women are experiencing manipulation and false teaching. In the study of more than twenty thousand married women previously mentioned, researchers discovered that 34.8 percent of women feel guilty (this study defines guilt as shame) when they turn down their husbands, because these women believe they are obligated to have sex with their husband in order to prevent them from sexually sinning.[76] These women lack an understanding of the beauty of sex as described in the Bible, and instead they experience sexual shame because as wives, they do not fulfill their "duties" in relation to their husbands as communicated by the religious community.[77] As these examples show, bad teachings and gender stereotypes run rampant inside Christian churches.[78] Research has demonstrated

---

72. Carnes, *Don't Call It Love*, 307.
73. Stringer, *Unwanted*, 62.
74. Neill, "Problematic Sexual Beliefs," 61.
75. Stringer, *Unwanted*, 62.
76. Gregoire et al., *Great Sex Rescue*, 168.
77. McClintock, *Shame-Less Lives*, 138–39.
78. Corey Farr is a single man who has written on gender roles in the church. He explains the core gender-role belief as this: "Singles are not

that women who attend churches with traditional gender roles experience more shame than people who do not.[79] In fact, research shows that when women believe these false teachings, like believing they are obligated to have sex with their husbands whenever their husbands want sex, they are 37 percent more likely to experience sexual pain (possibly from vaginismus) and 29 percent less likely to experience orgasm.[80] Women need to be taught correct Bible interpretation and that they are not ultimately responsible for their husbands' thoughts or actions.

When stereotypes are deeply engrained in the church's teachings, women feel uncomfortable confessing their sexual struggles. Research reveals that when struggling with a porn addiction, more practicing Christian young men than women reach out to their pastor for help.[81] Josh McDowell, an apologist who is passionate about addressing the church's porn epidemic, states that female "reticence may be due in part to the social stigma associated with female porn use or to the fact that most pastors are men, which adds a layer of social and sexual complexity to the pastor-parishioner relationship."[82] If only men are pastors, women feel sexual shame when they admit their sexual issues to their pastors and also if they remain silent. Not hearing stories from women continues the common myth pastors believe—that "only men struggle"— so they refrain from including women and sexuality in sermons.

'complete' men/women until marriage" (Farr, "Gender Roles," para. 7). Unbiblical teaching about gender roles hurts singles in a variety of ways: "It unintentionally shames those of us (such as myself) whose personalities and interests deviate from many of the culturally-imposed norms of 'masculinity,'" and "it reinforces the over-sexualization of all male-female relationships. Because gender roles are always taught within the context of marriage, men and women (especially singles) can't enjoy deep and appropriate friendships without raising eyebrows" (Farr, "Gender Roles," paras. 8–9).

79. Hottenstein, "Femininity, Masculinity, Gender, and the Role of Shame," 25.

80. Gregoire et al., *Great Sex Rescue*, 161.

81. McDowell, *Porn Phenomenon*, 101.

82. McDowell, *Porn Phenomenon*, 101.

Silence or false messages reinforce the belief that women do not struggle with sexual issues.

When women experience religious messages that are unbiblical or are slightly twisted from the truth, women are at risk for experiencing sexual shame and a distortion of God's design for sexuality. In one study, researchers interviewed women who were raised Protestant or Catholic, asking about their understandings of sexuality and spirituality. The study revealed that the women divided sex from the spirit, and their view of this dichotomy led to fear and shame regulating their sexuality. And the fear and shame had a detrimental effect on their overall sexual, emotional, and spiritual well-being.[83] Such a body-spirit divide could result from the devaluing of women in the church, which leads to a lack of understanding one's identity as a Christian woman.

Christian women also experience sexual shame around issues of abortion. Attached to their shame is an added religious abortion stigma different from that experienced by the general population.[84] The church has historically been concerned for the unborn, but it has generally expressed less concern for those bearing the unwanted children. In contrast, one often sees the casting of shame on the victims of possible sexual crimes, such as rape, who got pregnant outside of marriage. The late theologian Stanley Grenz believed "the Christian community ought to minister God's acceptance and healing to mothers in distress, counseling them toward non-abortion options, if these are feasible, within an atmosphere of understanding, but standing beside them no matter what decisions they ultimately make."[85] If the church loved like Jesus loved, there would be less sexual shame among Christian women.

When a Christian woman understands her body as something other than having God-given dignity, sexual shame sneaks in. Sellers, as a licensed marriage and family therapist and certified sex therapist, regularly sees Christian women with body shame and sexual shame. She discovered that many young Christian

---

83. Blum, "Women, Sex, and God," 220.
84. Frohwirth et al., "Managing Religion and Morality," 382.
85. Grenz, *Sexual Ethics*, 160.

Previous Research and Literature Review

women experience such high levels of sexual shame that it actually prohibits them from experiencing erotic feelings.[86] Sellers labels this phenomenon "religious sexual shame" and explains that religious sexual shame is "promoted by particular religious messages about the sexual self, innate sexual desire, natural sexual curiosity, natural sexual thoughts, and sexual actions."[87] One example that she presents is of a child touching themselves and a parent catching them and reacting with anger or saying, "God wouldn't want you touching your body that way."[88] Such negative messaging trains children at a young age to think God dislikes their sexuality, even though God created it as a good thing. If the child sees a horrified face or hears an angry tone from the parent, the child will unintentionally establish a connection between sexual behaviors and shame.[89]

Christian women also experience sexual shame when they struggle with same-sex attraction. Dr. Christopher Yuan, a Christian speaker and author on faith and sexuality and a professor at Moody Bible Institute, explains that those with same-sex temptations are burdened with shame, because they feel that they are unworthy of God's love and grace.[90] The shame they experience causes them to hide from rather than interact with others. When churches fail to provide a safe place for same-sex-attracted people to talk about their experiences, youth turn to the world. Yuan explains, "Our youth often seek answers from the world since they expect to be judged by the church simply for experiencing same-sex attractions. They fear no one will understand them. It's no wonder many end up having an incorrect understanding of sexuality."[91] No wonder many women are leaving the church.

Christian women struggle with sexual shame, but how do they find freedom? Helping them do so is the purpose of this

86. Sellers, *Sex*, xxiv.
87. Sellers, *Sex*, xxiv.
88. Sellers, *Sex*, xxiv–xxv.
89. McClintock, *Shame-Less Lives*, 133.
90. Yuan, *Holy Sexuality*, 72.
91. Yuan, *Holy Sexuality*, 163.

study. By correlating the surveys of Christian women who have experienced a degree of freedom from their sexual shame, readers will discover how they found freedom and how others can be free. In addition, this study will add to the growing body of research related to areas of shame, sexual shame, and sexuality.

Freedom from Sexual Shame

Women have found freedom from sexual shame in many ways. This section will look at a few examples of ways women have experienced healing from sexual shame, then will look at unhelpful ways to remove sexual shame, and lastly, the section will focus on the three hypotheses of this research project.

Twelve-step groups, Christian or secular therapy with nonjudgmental relationships, group therapy, mindfulness practice, and changing negative thought patterns and emotions (cognitive behavioral therapy) are practical means through which women can begin to find freedom from sexual shame.[92] In cognitive behavioral therapy (CBT), when treating sexual addiction, psychologists define shame as "the painful feeling of being unacceptable. It is the core effect of narcissistic damage; it is a driver of the addictive cycle and high levels of shame are often associated with addictive compulsive behavior."[93] During CBT, when patients experience shame following an unwanted sexual behavior, they use terms like "loser" or "flawed," which creates a mindset that can lead to additional acting out.[94] To escape the shame, people will try to produce a sense of numbness by turning to other things, in this case unwanted sexual behaviors. Psychologists performing CBT therapy have found that in their treatment programs, "a reduction in shame coincides with a reduction in acting-out behaviors."[95] One research study of women who experienced high

---

92. Birchard, *Compulsive Sexual Behaviour*, 155.
93. Birchard, *Compulsive Sexual Behaviour*, 9.
94. Birchard, *Compulsive Sexual Behaviour*, 18, 49.
95. Birchard, *Compulsive Sexual Behaviour*, 9.

levels of sexual shame due to abuse found that dialectical behavior therapy (DBT) helped decrease shame significantly.[96] Treatments such as CBT and DBT as well as others provide practical ways to remove sexual shame by uncovering the roots of shame. Instead of trying to remove temptations and sexual desires, counselors and therapists can uncover the root issue of what is triggering clients. Women will find freedom from sexual shame through the healing of sexual wounds.

A pastor, professor, and psychologist who specializes in shame recovery asserts that the only way to remove shame is to replace shame consciousness with intentional grace.[97] Understanding God's grace is key to finding freedom from sexual shame, which often helps women understand forgiveness. For situations that do not involve abuse, the woman can ask God for forgiveness and forgive herself for her unwanted sexual behaviors in order to find healing. Ferree explains that the process of forgiving oneself is helpful for sexual addicts stuck in sexual shame:

> Our core belief that we are horrible, terrible people hamstrings our ability to extend grace to ourselves. It's easier to beat ourselves up than it is to walk in newness of life. Living in shame, after all, is one of the results from our trauma. Core healing means that we exchange our identity of refuse for one of redemption. We become women redeemed from sexual shame by the power of God's forgiveness toward us and by our forgiveness of ourselves and others.[98]

Women will better be able to extend themselves grace if they see their Christian leaders and pastors leading with humility. Recovery from sexual shame requires humility. One study found that "the underlying difficulty seems to be how to counteract a wrong perception of self without shaming the person as a whole."[99] The study concludes, "If Christian communities would actively seek

---

96. Görg et al., "Trauma-Related Emotions," 1–12.
97. McClintock, *Shame-Less Lives*, 11.
98. Ferree, *No Stones*, 221–22.
99. Arens, "Bound to Shame," 187.

to diminish toxic shame and its effects, a necessary precondition would be to consciously adopt a similar attitude as twelve-step communities about their membership: nobody is ever excluded for whatever somebody has done or is still doing."[100] The conclusion of this study presents a powerful message that can be summed up with Slattery's statement "We are all sexually broken."[101] Understanding that people are all sexually broken will help leaders lead with humility. An additional study concluded that the following are the top five ways to find freedom from shame:

1. "Understand the origin of the shame and its function in the addictive system."
2. "Differentiate between shame and guilt."
3. "Identify the defenses utilized to deny the painful feelings created by the shame."
4. "Utilize specific shame reduction strategies at critical points in the treatment process."
5. "Change negative core beliefs that reinforce shame."[102]

Scholar Stephen Pattison's research takes similar truths and applies them to the church. He believes that the church could help people find freedom from shame by making these changes: using inclusive language, training on the effects of shame, and developing social ways of actively affirming individuals and groups.[103] Sellers has a four-step process for helping people heal from religious sexual shame—a process she outlines as "frame, name, claim, and aim," defined below:

1. "*Frame* involves a client receiving the framework of sex education that they have never had."
2. "*Name* is the process of getting their story heard and accepted by someone who cares for them."

---

100. Arens, "Bound to Shame," 188.
101. Slattery, *Rethinking Sexuality*, 78–79.
102. Adams and Robinson, "Shame Reduction," 25.
103. Pattison, *Shame*, 294.

3. "*Claim* has to do with claiming one's body and all of its wonderful, unique aspects, and undoing any harmful messages inherited from religion and culture."

4. "*Aim* is the process of writing a new story of where they are going, what they now believe, and what their legacy is going to become."[104]

Sellers states that these four processes may need to be repeated and revisited, but that in time, her clients have experienced freedom from shame.[105]

Lastly, Jay Stringer, a licensed mental health counselor, ordained minister, and speaker on the subject of unwanted sexual behavior, surveyed more than 3,800 men and women who had sought guidance in the midst of sexual brokenness. He found that shame was the most consistent key driver of unwanted sexual behavior.[106] He discovered that one of the most important tools to help clients is to disarm the power of shame.[107] He encourages clients to commit to healing the wounds that are causing the shame. Stringer explains the ultimate defeat of shame as "when the very experiences that attempted to convince you that you were unwanted become the sources of greatest joy of being loved."[108] Stringer provides three ways to find healing:

1. "Talk to a trusted guide (a therapist, pastor, or sponsor) about the specific stories where you harbor shame."

2. "Write a story from your childhood about when shame seemed particularly present in your life."

3. "Spend time reflecting on it with a guide. As you reflect on the story, where do you feel it in your body? Did shame occur because you experienced pleasure? Did someone shame

---

104. Sellers, *Sex*, 81.
105. Sellers, *Sex*, 81.
106. Stringer, *Unwanted*, 143.
107. Stringer, *Unwanted*, 143.
108. Stringer, *Unwanted*, 146.

you, or were you all alone when something painful occurred? How do you think this story affects you today?"[109]

Stringer states that all of the answers to the questions teach about what parts of one's story need healing. Lastly, he concludes by encouraging his clients to continue educating themselves about shame and its connection with their unwanted sexual behaviors.[110]

Unhelpful Ways to Remove Sexual Shame

Recently, some authors writing about women experiencing sexual shame have reached differing conclusions about how one experiences freedom. The problem is that there is partial truth in all of their books, which is confusing for women who are hurting due to sexual shame and are looking for answers. The first example is research done by Linda Kay Klein. After researching and interviewing countless women who were negatively affected by the purity culture in churches, she explained the impact as follows: "Evangelical Christianity's sexual purity movement is traumatizing many girls and maturing women haunted by sexual and gender-based anxiety, fear, and physical experiences that sometimes mimic the symptoms of post-traumatic stress disorder (PTSD)."[111] In her writings, Klein notes stories of nightmares, panic attacks, and paranoia that were common to many of the women she interviewed.

Klein correctly concludes that the purity culture did nurture the development of shame. Many women felt powerless and worthless, and they lived with fear of abandonment that caused them to hide and feel ashamed of themselves. Consequently, they withdrew from others.[112] Failing to meet the perfect standards from the purity culture made women believe that they were bad for being sexual beings. Klein explained the impact that the shameful

---

109. Stringer, *Unwanted*, 147.
110. Stringer, *Unwanted*, 148.
111. Klein, *Pure*, 8.
112. Klein, *Pure*, 15.

purity-culture messages had on women's bodies, including her own. She said, "Rather than seek help, we bury our shaming experiences deep in our bodies, where they are held similarly to trauma."[113] Pushing down sexual feelings and repressing memories will deeply affect the physical sexual response systems. If a woman feels shame every time she has sexual thoughts or experiences sexual desires, she is repeatedly firing neurons at the same time. And the neuron overload will result in sex and shame becoming difficult to disconnect in the brain, because a woman's neural pathways have been physically altered.[114] While Klein is correct on the problem, she is incorrect on the solution. Klein's solution is to throw out Scripture and sexual integrity and embrace the freedom to do anything one desires. Both extremes, the purity culture and Klein's solution, are far from Sexual Discipleship and actually create more sexual shame for Christian women that may result in their walking away from the church or faith.

Another example of misleading research is that published by Nadia Bolz-Weber, who claims to be "pro-porn" and "sex positivity." The purpose of sex positivity is, she says, "to counter messages and attitudes about sex that are based on shame."[115] Bolz-Weber believes that porn can help remove sexual shame. The data suggests that the sex-positive movement is growing, as "two in five adults 18 and older agree that sexual images and situations in media are important for showing people how to be positive about sex."[116] When porn is one's sex education, the student will have a false and inadequate education that actually creates more sexual shame than removes it. Bolz-Weber sees the negatives that the purity culture created and argues, "We should not be more loyal to an idea, a doctrine or an interpretation of a Bible verse than we are to people. If the teachings of the church are harming the bodies and spirits of people, we should rethink those teachings."[117]

113. Klein, *Pure*, 15.
114. Klein, *Pure*, 189.
115. McDowell, *Porn Phenomenon*, 77.
116. McDowell, *Porn Phenomenon*, 77.
117. Bolz-Weber, *Shameless*, 5.

Bolz-Weber's opinions do not align. She is pro-porn to remove shame, but then she makes statements that those hurting watch more porn. She explains the trends she's seen in her work as a pastor: "The more someone was exposed to religious messages about controlling their desires, avoiding sexual thoughts, and not lusting in their hearts, the less likely they are to be integrated physically, emotionally, sexually, and spiritually. I've also noticed that the less integrated physically, emotionally, sexually, and spiritual someone is, the more pornography they tend to consume."[118] Bolz-Weber removes Scripture from the conversation and goes to an opposite extreme from the purity narrative to create a new sexual ethic.

Finally, a third recent project that contributes to false teachings about freedom from shame was written by therapist and theologian Matthias Roberts. He believes that the only way to experience freedom from sexual shame is to embrace a biblical view that sex before marriage is okay and and encourages same-sex relationships.[119] When he was growing up, his church had an unbiblical view of sex and gender and embraced the purity-culture messages of manhood and womanhood.

The problem with Roberts's book and the others mentioned is that they all contain truth. For example, Roberts asserts that the best way to find freedom from shame is to "learn how to recognize shame and bring it into the light."[120] He also states that freedom comes through community: "Shame fighting cannot happen without the presence of other people. We simply can't fight shame alone."[121] Roberts sees the correct problems, but he offers only partially correct solutions. Yet, contra Roberts, the solution to freeing people from sexual shame is not to throw out God's word because of the incorrect ways Christians have interpreted it and applied it.

Of all the possible solutions for sexual shame, this research project has found that the evidence validates three

---

118. Bolz-Weber, *Shameless*, 139–40.
119. Roberts, *Beyond Shame*.
120. Roberts, *Beyond Shame*, 4.
121. Roberts, *Beyond Shame*, 9.

specific hypotheses as the most powerful for Christian women to find healing from sexual shame. Hypothesis 1: Christian women will identify understanding the love and grace of God as a key factor in finding freedom from sexual shame. Hypothesis 2: Christian women will identify being known in biblical community as a key factor in finding freedom from sexual shame. Hypothesis 3: Christian women will identify learning a biblical teaching of sexuality through Sexual Discipleship as a key factor in finding freedom from sexual shame. This research has shown that these three hypotheses work best when used together with Sexual Discipleship in order to stop sexual shame from developing and bring healing for those with sexual shame.

Hypothesis 1

Hypothesis 1 states, "Christian women will identify understanding the love and grace of God as a key factor in finding freedom from sexual shame."

Before the surveys and interviews were conducted, three hypotheses were chosen. Similar statements have been researched by previous literature in the lives of men and women. The hurting can understand God's character to find freedom from sexual shame. Stringer states that "the God of the universe is neither surprised by nor ashamed of the sexual behavior we participate in."[122] In fact, "his heart is to exchange beauty for ashes, joy for mourning, and praise for despair. There is no depth of shame that the love of God cannot reach. There is no story he cannot redeem" (Isa 61:3).[123] The way believers can begin to understand God's character, his love and grace, is by looking to the cross. When people understand God's grace to them, they can give grace to themselves. Research has shown that shame could be due to a misunderstanding of the gospel.[124] When people understand that God loves them so much

---

122. Stringer, *Unwanted*, xx.
123. Stringer, *Unwanted*, xx.
124. Perry, *Addicted to Lust*, 15.

that he sent Jesus to die for them, they can experience healing. A part of this hypothesis is understanding what it means for one's identity to be a Christ follower. When one understands what it means for her identity to be in Christ and how he has already experienced and taken on her shame, then she can walk in freedom. Understanding one's identity in Christ begins with the life of Jesus. Jesus was born to an unwed mother and was a child of Nazareth. As he got older, Jesus frequently spent time with women, touched lepers, and then hung on a cross. When women experience sexual shame, they need to understand that Jesus has empathy and love for them. God's love heals people from sexual shame.

When women are in crisis, they can have comfort knowing that Jesus went through trauma for them. The prophet Isaiah, speaking for God, states, "I offered my back to those who beat me, my cheeks to those who pulled out my beard; I did not hide my face from mocking and spitting" (Isa 50:6). The words are prophetic, and one can recognize the Christ in them. Indeed, Jesus understands shame on a personal level. He did not hide his face from the shame; he did not cover himself or run from it; he stared the shame right in the face.[125] Jesus can relate to suffering. Nelson concurs, stating, "Freedom comes as I fix my eyes on Jesus, realizing that the cross is the focal point where my sin is forgiven, and my shame is covered."[126] Women can understand that Jesus's death on the cross covered their shame. Jesus is the answer to finding freedom from shame, because he took on the shame of the world in the most shameful death possible. The crucifixion of Jesus is the embodiment of shame.[127] Langberg states this beautifully: "Set on high for all to see—naked, struck, beard plucked out, spit upon, humiliated, and erected on one of the most shaming and torturous instruments of death in the history of the world. He was shamed by the world he had made. He became shame, embodied it. All could see—he did not hide."[128] Jesus understands shame in

---

125. Langberg, *Suffering*, 139.
126. Nelson, *Unashamed*, 114.
127. Rutledge, *Crucifixion*, 96.
128. Langberg, *Suffering*, 138.

a deeper way than anyone has ever experienced it. Knowing that a Christian's identity is in Christ and what he did on the cross frees people from shame.

Christ comforts and brings justice. Jesus's death on the cross frees people from shame by his blood. In the words of Holcomb and Holcomb: "Because of the cross, we can be fully exposed, because God no longer identifies us by what we have done."[129] Jesus willingly clothed himself with man and woman's dishonor on the cross. No one can cover their own shame. Only when they have faith in Jesus do they receive honor, as he takes on their shame. From his death, people receive forgiveness, joy, and freedom—the opposite of shame. They receive redemption for the things done to them or against them. They experience a cleansing of sins and experience a righteousness that only Christ can provide. No longer are they defiled, filthy, or stained, but they are made pure. Because of the cross, they can walk free, because Christ set them free. This grace is a far greater motivator for sexual behavior than the law or rules ever were, meaning that people try to find freedom by their own strength, but their doing so leaves them emptier and with more shame.[130] When women are compelled and motivated by the love and grace of Christ, that is when true freedom happens. Ferree, a former sex addict who found healing from addiction and sexual shame, states, "The best part of the healing process was coming to know a God I'd never imagined—a God of pursuing grace who was fully able to meet my needs."[131] Ferree traded rules-based religion for a relationship-based religion with Jesus. The relationship with Jesus still has rules to protect and guide, but they flow out of the heart and lead to flourishing. God did not create people as robots. God created humans with choices and hearts to obey him out of an overflowing love for him. She explains that "grace motivates in a way that shame cannot, and I longed to respond to God's love with obedience, rather than perform out of fear."[132]

129. Holcomb and Holcomb, *Rid of My Disgrace*, 102–3.
130. Hirsch, *Redeeming Sex*, 205.
131. Ferree, *No Stones*, 21.
132. Ferree, *No Stones*, 21.

Understanding God's love and grace can be displayed practically as growing in a stronger relationship with God and Jesus. Author Cynthia Humbert says, "Until we clearly understand who God truly is, how passionately he loves us, and how deeply he desires to restore us into right relationship with him, we will continue to search for fulfillment in unsafe places."[133] Knowing and experiencing the love of God will be the only way to experience deep fulfillment, but misunderstanding God's love can lead to confusion. Some people would argue that God's love would accept and promote certain sexual behaviors. Slattery counters, explaining, "A mischaracterization of God's love will inevitably taint our understanding of biblical sexuality. Much of the confusion we see related to sexual issues among Christians is rooted in how we misrepresent God's love."[134] One popular modern interpretation of God's love is that the Almighty wants people to feel happy, complete, and fully accepted, but this eliminates sin.[135] Understanding that people are sinners is what helps people better understand God's love. The apostle Paul, writing to the church at Rome, said, "But God demonstrates his own love for us in this: While we were still sinners, Christ died for us" (Rom 5:8). God's love provides a way to be holy, forgiven, redeemed, restored, and freed from sexual shame. If believers do not know and experience this kind of love, they could easily experience sexual shame. In fact, Slattery says, "The sexual confusion we see in our culture is rooted in spiritual confusion," as "every sexual question begins and ends with questions about God."[136] This confusion is part of the reason authors like Klein, Bolz-Weber, and Roberts have incorrect responses to how believers find freedom from sexual shame: they have an incorrect view of God.

One author who was sexually abused as a child and experienced sexual shame describes the moment that changed her life, when she began to find freedom: "I saw his [Jesus's] love for me,

---

133. Humbert, *Deceived by Shame*, 28.
134. Slattery, *Rethinking Sexuality*, 43.
135. Slattery, *Rethinking Sexuality*, 44.
136. Slattery, *Rethinking Sexuality*, 36.

his unwillingness for me to suffer alone, and his judgment against the abuse ... his 'no' to the shame and sin that scarred my life."[137] Her new understanding began to change her identity. She began to understand that she was not alone in her suffering. She said, "Jesus's experience of the cross has everything to do with our wounds and our sorrows. His resurrection from the dead is more than a creed we recite. It is a living power that lifts us out of the black holes of our lives, that heals our wounds, that removes our shame."[138] Jesus already died for shame. Right before Jesus died, he said, "It is finished!" (John 19:30). Believers can either live chained to their shame, or they can remember that Jesus already finished his work on the cross. Finding freedom from sexual shame requires believers to understand what it means to be in Christ. Believers can trust that one day, "we will be clothed in the honor of Jesus Christ when we stand before God in all his glory. Shame will be eradicated forever. No more hiding."[139] Experiencing healing compels believers to understand God's love, grace, and their identity in Christ. This love from God and love of God through others is one of the cures for sexual shame.[140] When one better understands God's love and grace for his children and their identity in Christ, they will begin to find healing from sexual shame.

Hypothesis 2

Hypothesis 2 states, "Christian women will identify being known in biblical community as a key factor in finding freedom from sexual shame."

God created people with desires to be fully loved and fully known. Experiencing being fully loved and fully known in the context of community is necessary for healing from sexual shame.[141]

137. Heath, *Healing the Wounds*, 9.
138. Heath, *Healing the Wounds*, 10.
139. Nelson, *Unashamed*, 171.
140. Birchard, *Compulsive Sexual Behaviour*, 60.
141. Thompson, *Soul of Shame*, 133.

First, the term "biblical community" will be defined, followed by a look to Scripture and Jesus as examples. Jerry Bridges, author of *True Community*, explains that to find the definitions of biblical community, one can study the Greek. Bridges explains the Greek word *koinōnia* found in the New Testament most often means fellowship, but he explains that different translations of the word into English include "participation, partnership, sharing."[142] Bridges points out that the first mention of *koinōnia* in the New Testament is at Pentecost.[143] The author of Acts, presumably Luke, explains that new believers "devoted themselves to the apostles' teaching and to the fellowship, to the breaking of bread and to prayer" (Acts 2:42). These new believers were focused on sharing a life together in fellowship through relationships—biblical community. To summarize *koinōnia* in the most basic way, Bridges states, "It is sharing a common life with other believers—a life that, as John says, we share with God the Father and God the Son. It is a relationship, not an activity."[144] Nelson explains the calling of biblical community: "In Christ-formed community, we are called to practice shame-eradicating love" in order to counter people's deepest fear—"that I am not worthy of another's love and acceptance."[145] Nelson also provides a list of Scriptures that explain the purpose of biblical community:

> Love one another (John 13:34; 1 Pet 1:22; 1 John 3:11, 23; 4:7, 11–12; 2 John 1:5). Clothe yourself with humility toward one another (1 Pet 5:5). Stop passing judgment on one another (Rom 14:13). Accept one another (Rom 15:7). Encourage one another and build each other up (1 Thess 5:11; Heb 3:13; 10:25). Speak the truth to one another (Eph 4:25; Col 3:8–9). Confess your sins to one another (Jas 5:16). Serve one another (Gal 5:13; 1 Pet

---

142. Bridges, *True Community*, 1.
143. Bridges, *True Community*, 2.
144. Bridges, *True Community*, 2.
145. Nelson, *Unashamed*, 52.

4:10). Comfort one another (1 Thess 4:18; 5:14). Be kind and compassionate to one another (Eph 4:32).[146]

Additionally, one can look to Jesus as an example of loving others. The *Pericope Adulterae* attributed to the apostle John is an account of an adulterous woman being brought before Jesus. When he sees her, he looks her in the eyes, sees her fears and pain, knows her story, and yet he loves her unconditionally (John 8:1–11). About this story, Reinhart states, "People never really change very deeply until someone catches them in their shame and is not appalled."[147] The woman in this story was experiencing sexual shame, and yet Jesus was not appalled. Jesus knew her fully and loved her fully. Women need the help of others (community) to hear and see over and over that they are loved, cared for, and not ruined. And this experience will break the shame.[148] Healing from sexual shame requires healing in relationships with others. The problem is, however, that many people do not have a safe community. Stringer found that 59 percent of people he interviewed struggling with unwanted sexual behavior did not feel as though they had someone to talk to, and only 20 percent pursued someone they could talk to when they were struggling with sexual behavior.[149] The author believed that once people experienced sexual shame, they believed they had no one to talk to, and this aloneness resulted in isolation.

Since isolation is one of shame's primary methods of destruction, believers can surround themselves with trustworthy people in order to "loosen shame's grip on life by living transparently as often as possible."[150] Instead of moving away from one another, Christian women can move toward one another and connect in community. Sharing the most shameful parts of one's story can be scary. Despite humans' tendency to isolate when they feel ashamed,

---

146. Nelson, *Unashamed*, 48.
147. Rinehart, *Soul of a Woman*, 94.
148. Thompson, *Soul of Shame*, 147.
149. Stringer, *Unwanted*, 206.
150. Thompson, *Soul of Shame*, 137.

God created his children for relationship. Believers can walk in the light, be a part of fellowship and community, confess sin to one another, and experience forgiveness. Then, they can experience freedom (1 John 1:7–9). Research has suggested that "the ultimate treatment goal for sex addicts is to master the experience of bonding and attaching in enduring and trusting intimate connections with others."[151] It is only through trusted intimate relationships that one can begin to find healing. In fact, Stringer found in his clients a 22 percent reduction in heavy porn viewing for those that told their story with someone in biblical community compared to those who had no one to talk to.[152] Sharing their story and being met with love was the key for healing.

Honesty about oneself in the context of these relationships is essential. Such honesty includes confession and is a part of biblical community. Brown explains the beauty of community that conforms to a biblical vision of confession: "The Lord calls us to walk in the light, to confess our sins to fellow believers, but to do that we must create communities absent of shame and judgment, where our brothers and sisters can confess and repent of their sin and be met with love, acceptance and help." [153] Such a community is the opposite of the "don't ask, don't tell," or silence, approach to sexuality, which keeps people stuck in the cycle of shame.[154] Confessing sins by bringing them into the light with another safe and trusted person removes sexual shame. Confessing relationships are marked with trust, honesty, and safety. Grant explains the importance of confession: "The shame and stigma often attached to sexual sin and dysfunction tends to drive people into isolation and hiding. Indeed, a trusted mentoring relationship may be the only place where their issues can be confessed and addressed."[155]

A biblical community creates a sense of belonging for women struggling with sexual shame. A sense of belonging to a biblical

---

151. Adams and Robinson, "Shame Reduction," 23.
152. Stringer, *Unwanted*, 207.
153. McDowell, *Porn Phenomenon*, 123.
154. Grant, *Divine Sex*, 114.
155. Grant, *Divine Sex*, 210.

Previous Research and Literature Review

community will encourage, support, guide, and help such a woman find freedom. In one research study, Brown found that to develop shame resilience, one must start by "decreasing the feelings of being trapped, powerless, and isolated and to increase the opportunities to experience empathy by increasing connection, power, and freedom."[156] Brown believes that a combination of empathy, power, and connection will create freedom. Brown explains how to reduce shame in all of her work. In a TED Talk, she defines shame as "the fear of disconnection" and states that the "antidote to shame is empathy and vulnerability."[157] The right kind of connection results in healing.

Brown explains in her research that healthy "connection" provided support, shared experiences, and "allowed the women to move away from the social/cultural trappings of the shame web by working with others to redefine what is valuable and important."[158] Connecting allowed the women to lose the sense of aloneness in their experiences. In fact, Brown observed that participants in her research study said that "being with others who have had similar experiences" or "talking with people who've been there," were two of the most helpful steps in their healing.[159] Yuan similarly argues that "comfort comes from knowing we are not alone. We need to be honest and transparent with trusting others about our struggles with unchosen and often ongoing temptations."[160] Thus, to alleviate shame, leaders must help connect and restore women through community and help them understand that they are not alone in their struggles.

One way to connect women is through sharing stories. Sharing one's story and experiencing empathy and vulnerability has a strong correlation with reducing stigmatization and shame.[161] Stringer, who helps many clients with unwanted sexual behaviors,

---

156. Brown, "Shame Resilience Theory," 41.
157. Brown, "Power of Vulnerability."
158. Brown, "Shame Resilience Theory," 47.
159. Brown, "Shame Resilience Theory," 51.
160. Yuan, *Holy Sexuality*, 72.
161. McClintock, *Shame-Less Lives*, 118.

encourages his clients to tell their shameful stories to him in therapy. He believes that by sharing the formative experiences of one's life, especially childhood, his clients can uncover loneliness, pain, sexual arousal, and secrecy to point out why he or she has unwanted sexual behavior as an adult.[162] Stringer states, "Our struggles are not random or capricious. There are always reasons. If we want to find freedom, it begins by identifying your specific reasons."[163] Stringer himself experienced freedom from shame surrounding his unwanted sexual behaviors when he told his story to his therapist. As he spoke, "blankets of shame and condemnation lifted because my therapist was inviting me not primarily to stop my lust but to engage the sexual story I was set up for."[164] Other therapists use an approach similar to that of Stringer. They have seen that when working with women, "the need to turn their problems inside out is ever more pressing when it is clear that their experience is structured by repertoires of shame, blame and harming."[165] One way to encourage such storytelling is through narrative therapy—viewing people's experiences as narratives as a way of unravelling the stories people bring with them.[166] To make sense of the present, therapists help people understand the past.[167] Sharing one's story is a delicate dance, because narratives could easily be met with rejection, which would lead to more shame. The more people speak about their deep shame wounds, the greater chance for further wounding, but also the greater chance for healing.

For an environment to be safe enough to share one's story, there must be empathy. In her research, Brown discovered the power of empathy as the opposite of experiencing shame. She explained, "Women with high levels of shame resilience were both givers and receivers of empathy."[168] She asked them to write

162. Stringer, *Unwanted*, xxi.
163. Stringer, *Unwanted*, xxii.
164. Stringer, *Unwanted*, xxiv.
165. Reavey and Gough, "Dis/Locating Blame," 340.
166. Reavey and Gough, "Dis/Locating Blame," 340.
167. Reavey and Gough, "Dis/Locating Blame," 340.
168. Brown, *I Thought*, 32.

examples of how they found freedom from shame, and they described situations in which they felt safe to talk about their story with an empathetic person. They responded in the healing power of hearing someone respond with "I understand—I've been there" or "That's happened to me too," or "It's okay, you're normal."[169] In Brown's research, participants reported that in experiencing an empathetic response to their shame experience, their sense of connection was often increased, restored, and strengthened.[170] Brown concluded, "The comfort comes from recognizing that we are not alone in our struggles; we aren't the only ones. One reason shame is so powerful is its ability to make us feel alone."[171]

Carnes's approach is congruent with that of Brown. Carnes notes that sexual addicts find freedom from shame through sharing their stories with other addicts: "On hearing others' stories, addicts understand that they are not unique, not misfits or perverts. And when they tell their own stories, they feel acceptance and care."[172] Exchanging stories with others reduces sexual shame. When women are given opportunities to be open and honest about their struggles, they are less likely to get stuck in shame.[173] Connection must be paired with mutual support, shared experiences, acceptance, and belonging.[174] Such pairing can take place one-on-one or in larger group settings.

For Christian women, the church can also provide community to help women find freedom from sexual shame. When the church embraces brokenness of others, people can experience the life-changing power of the gospel. The gospel's power will remove shame and allow all people to feel welcomed. Women need to belong, because that is how God created humans—in desperate need of community in order to thrive. Stockitt sums up perfectly the reason humans need others: "If God himself dwells within a

169. Brown, *I Thought*, 33.
170. Brown, "Shame Resilience Theory," 47.
171. Brown, *I Thought*, 9.
172. Carnes, *Don't Call It Love*, 233.
173. Brown, *I Thought*, 59.
174. Brown, *I Thought*, 47.

community of persons—Father, Son, and Holy Spirit—it is inconceivable that we could do otherwise."[175]

Hypothesis 3

Hypothesis 3 states, "Christian women will identify learning a biblical teaching of sexuality through Sexual Discipleship as a key factor in finding freedom from sexual shame."

Finally, women will experience freedom from sexual shame by receiving biblical teaching about sexuality through Sexual Discipleship. Slattery, the creator of the term "Sexual Discipleship," explains the process as follows: "Sexual discipleship begins with what we believe, translates to how we live, and results in what we pass on to the next generation."[176] When Christians are rooted in faith and God's word, they are not swayed by what North American culture says about sexuality. The problem is that such rooting is not true for many believers. Slattery observes that "the sexual behaviors and beliefs of many Christians are virtually indistinguishable from the world's."[177] When Christians follow the world's teaching of sexuality instead of Scripture, they easily could experience sexual shame. Christian women must understand what the Bible says about sexuality to live free from sexual shame. One pastor noted, "When the goodness of sexuality is affirmed from the pulpit and when sexual issues are brought into open forums, the congregation is on its way to shamelessness."[178] Sexual Discipleship focuses on the beauty of God's design for sexuality, which will remove sexual shame by pointing people to God's love. Slattery asks, "What if we could use every conversation about erotica and pornography to get to the heart of people? What if instead of focusing so much on prostitution, pornography, and premarital sex,

---

175. Stockitt, *Restoring the Shamed*, 41.
176. Slattery, *Rethinking Sexuality*, 31.
177. Slattery, *Rethinking Sexuality*, 29.
178. McClintock, *Shame-Less Lives*, 164.

we used these counterfeits as an on-ramp to explore how we all long for true intimacy and fulfillment?"[179]

Churches, families, and ministries need to reframe and change the conversations about sexuality. Instead of focusing on sex being "bad," leaders must embrace God's good design for sexuality. Freedom from sexual shame will begin (and sexual shame will possibly be prevented) when messages about biblical sexuality are a part of sex education and conversations at all ages. Parents and educators wishing to create healthier conversations will use accurate, non-drastic body terminology in a pleasant tone of voice to teach kids about their bodies.[180] Using correct terminology will allow safe places for conversation and may lower levels of sexual shame. When instructors proactively address sexuality issues across life spans, they will increase the congregation's comfort level with sexual subjects and remove sexual shame.[181]

Sexual shame stems from believing lies, which comes from bad theology. Most believers have no idea why God cares about their sexuality. God designed sex, erotic pleasure, and intimacy—it is nothing to be ashamed of. God created people with sexual desires to lead them to him.[182] Sex is not about legalistic morals that lack a basis in reality but about God, who is faithful and longs for a relationship with his children.[183] Hosea provides a great object lesson to illustrate God's faithfulness. Hosea records that God says to Israel, "I will betroth you to me forever; I will betroth you in righteousness and justice, in love and compassion. I will betroth you in faithfulness, and you will acknowledge the Lord" (Hos 2:19-20). God created sexuality and its goodness and, as the Healer, will redeem the brokenness of the world. The Lord loves his people and longs for a relationship with them. Sexual desires point people to God's love, but because of people's sinful flesh, worldly influences, and the accuser, people are pulled away from God.

179. Slattery, *Rethinking Sexuality*, 74.
180. Rough, *Beyond Birds and Bees*, 233.
181. McClintock, *Shame-Less Lives*, 155–56.
182. West, *Theology of the Body*, 63.
183. Jones, *Faithful*, 38.

Much has been said about unbiblical teaching and negative influences, but true biblical sexuality must focus on the good, God-created pleasure in sexuality to help people flourish. To start conversations about biblical sexuality, leaders may begin by explaining that God created people as sexual beings. In the garden of Eden, God blesses the man and woman with the exhortation to become one flesh (Gen 2:24). God's ultimate goal is oneness—two becoming one—this is God's beautiful design for sexuality so that his sons and daughters flourish.[184] The "one flesh" connection between man and woman in the garden is then described as "naked, and they felt no shame" (Gen 2:25). God created sex and gave it as a gift to unite two people as one. Scripture explains that the gift of sex is for the marriage bed. Sex is not a wicked thing, but unless sexuality is talked about as the gift that it is and addressed to women, women may feel shameful for sexual desires and curiosities. Part of teaching a biblical view of sexuality involves including women in these conversations.

The core of sexuality is a sign of God's goodness.[185] Believers must understand the theology of sex to find freedom. God is good and faithful, and God has blessed marriages with the gift of sex and frees singles to experience holy sexuality in singleness and chastity.[186] God can restore the brokenness and reclaim the lies. God can redeem his children to go back to the unashamed nakedness that is possible in the safety of covenant marriage and understand how to live a fulfilled life as a single sexual being intimately connected to Christ.[187]

To understand the biblical message of sexuality, West explains how it connects to the basic principles of the faith: "If we are made in the image of God as male and female (see Gen 1:27), and if joining in 'one flesh' is a 'profound mystery' that refers to Christ and the church (see Eph 5:31–32), then our understanding of the body, gender, and sexuality has a direct impact on our

---

184. Cutrer et al., *Sexual Intimacy in Marriage*, 281.
185. West, *Our Bodies*, 37.
186. Jones, *Faithful*, 53.
187. Jones, *Faithful*, 57.

understanding of God, Christ, and the church."[188] God's design for sexuality is not repressive but redemptive and a compelling vision of what it means to be male and female. When men and women engage in unwanted sexual behaviors, they experience sexual shame—leaders can actively change erroneous messages about sexuality to free people from sexual shame. Sexuality is a gift to be stewarded. And the goal of biblical sexuality is not marriage but becoming more like Christ. Slattery explains, "Our sexual desires and unmet cravings can propel us toward marriage, but ultimately they should propel us to the greater truth that we were made for eternal covenant."[189]

The Bible's teaching about sexuality is not a list of rules about sexuality, and false teaching that communicates sexuality as rule keeping is not Sexual Discipleship. Believers must start with a scriptural ethic of sex that begins with the totality of the Bible, the narrative of God's redeeming love, and humanity's attempt to reflect that love.[190] Hirsch explains the problem with divorcing particular verses from the totality of the Bible: "We are bound to dish out simplistic, theologically limp answers that neither satisfy nor make any real sense of the all-too-real human struggle. Seeing the Bible as a 'rule' book, especially related to sexuality, reflects not only on the God it points to but restricts our capacity to see his good intent in and through creation"[191] God created women as sexual beings, and the Creator's intention is a good thing. For example, an entire book in the Bible, Song of Songs, is devoted to sexual love. Eckert notes, "Our identity as sexual beings is foundational to how God has uniquely created us in his image. Becoming healthy, whole women means learning to listen to our uniquely female sexuality without denying, misusing, manipulating, worshiping, or rejecting it. We are called to celebrate the gift of our

---

188. West, *Our Bodies*, 4.
189. Slattery, *Rethinking Sexuality*, 56.
190. Winner, *Real Sex*, 30.
191. Hirsch, *Redeeming Sex*, 45–46.

sexuality."[192] To help women find freedom, believers can celebrate the gift of sexuality.

Conclusion

Chapter 2 looked at what the research and literature say about areas relating to sexual shame. Research and literature have validated the supposition that women will often experience freedom from sexual shame when they understand the love and grace of God, are known in biblical community, and learn biblical sexuality. Ferree describes what a woman will look like when she becomes free from sexual shame through the three categories:

> She allows God to cleanse her from the stains of her past. She sees herself as a new creation in Christ, beautiful and wholly pure. She guards her body as the temple of God and the bride of Christ. In purity, she practices surrender and selflessness. She seeks to be a living sacrifice to the Father who has redeemed her from sin and shame. A radical shift in her thinking and behavior happens as she embraces God's plan for healthy sexuality . . . She accepts God's boundaries for sexual expression as evidence of his desire of the best for his children. She expands her view of what it means to be a woman created in the image of God.[193]

Ferree portrays a women's restoration from sexual shame. The next chapter includes information about the procedure and research method for the research project.

---

192. Eckert, *Your Mother Never Told*, 129.
193. Ferree, *No Stones*, 257.

Chapter 3

Procedure and Research Method

Introduction

THE RESEARCH PROJECT ADDRESSED how women experience sexual shame and then explored how women find freedom from sexual shame. Chapter 3 will look at the problem statement, research question, hypotheses, research method and procedure, research instruments, and research subjects in order to discover how women find freedom from sexual shame.

Problem Statement and Research Question

The problem statement of this research project is that women experience sexual shame. This issue has led to a broad research question: How do women find freedom from sexual shame?

Hypotheses

The project has three hypotheses:

1. Christian women will identify understanding the love and grace of God as a key factor in finding freedom from sexual shame.

2. Christian women will identify being known in biblical community as a key factor in finding freedom from sexual shame.
3. Christian women will identify learning a biblical teaching of sexuality as a key factor in finding freedom from sexual shame.

Research Method and Procedures

The research project included administering a qualitative survey and a quantitative survey. Both surveys were conducted on SurveyMonkey. The qualitative survey was the best way to gather personal stories from women in order to gain a deep understanding of the sexual shame they experienced and the ways they experienced freedom. These surveys were deeper than the larger sample of the population from the quantitative surveys. Each completed survey was assigned an identification number upon receipt. The researcher read every answer to each open-ended question and was able to see broad patterns and themes among the participants. The quantitative survey was used in order to gather numerical data and evidence to get objective answers from the participants.

The information from the quantitative survey was tabulated and evaluated, and the results are reported in the form of this doctoral dissertation. The quantitative data from the survey was exported to a spreadsheet so that it could be sorted by various filters to look for correlations between answers to different questions and for any patterns among the different age groups. For example, using the filters on the spreadsheet, one could determine if women of different ages felt freer than the others. The results of these calculations and correlations will be presented in chapter 4.

Procedure and Research Method

Research Instruments

Qualitative Survey

The instrument for the qualitative survey is included as Appendix A. To develop the qualitative survey, the researcher brainstormed questions with peers and fellow Dallas Theological Seminary students. In the qualitative survey, the researcher asked open-ended questions to collect stories and learn how women have found freedom.

Quantitative Survey

To develop the quantitative survey, the researcher worked with a research ministry, Teleios. The survey anonymously surveyed Christian women using a mixed-method approach. In the quantitative survey, the questions used either the Likert scale or a multiple-choice option to collect data. The instrument is included as Appendix B.

Research Subjects

Qualitative Survey

The subjects for the research were found through the internet, specifically through the social media platforms Instagram, Facebook, and Twitter and an email marketing list on MailChimp. For the qualitative survey, the researcher received forty-four useable surveys, meaning that forty-four women checked yes for permission to use this survey in research. If a person did not check yes, their survey responses were deleted. The participants in the study were assured of the confidentiality of their responses, because the survey was anonymous.

The following questions and results from the survey are presented here to provide more information on the participants. The questions that provide results for the research question "How have women experienced sexual shame and how have they found freedom from sexual shame?" will be included in the next chapter.

The ages of the forty-four participants, all of whom marked yes in response to the question "Are you a follower of Jesus Christ?" were as follows:

- 19–22 years old: 1
- 23–30 years old: 17
- 31–40 years old: 14
- 41–50 years old: 7
- 51–65 years old: 4
- 66 or older: 1

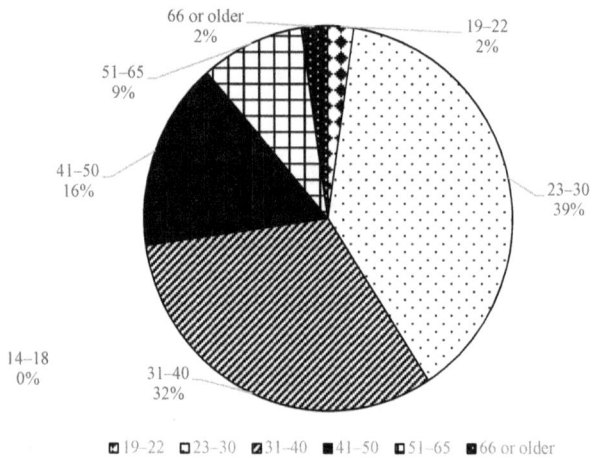

Figure 1. Age of Participants (Qualitative Survey)

Figure 1 shows that those who were twenty-three to thirty years old made up the biggest percentage at 38.64 percent, followed by those thirty-one to forty years old, who made up 31.82 percent.

Procedure and Research Method

Quantitative Survey

For the quantitative survey, also anonymous, 1,090 responses were received, with a 100 percent question-completion rate, averaging at four minutes and thirty seconds to complete the survey. These research subjects were gathered through the same social media platforms and email list. All 1,090 participants answered yes to the first question: "Are you a female who gives me permission to use this survey in my research project and future writing?" Of the 1,090 participants, their ages were as follows:

- 14–18 years old: 16
- 19–22 years old: 93
- 23–30 years old: 332
- 31–40 years old: 335
- 41–50 years old: 178
- 51–65 years old: 119
- 66 or older: 17

Figure 2. Age of Participants (Quantitative Survey)

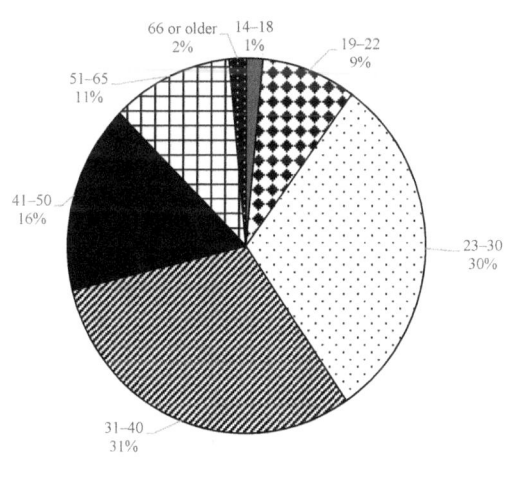

Figure 2 shows that those who were thirty-one to forty years old made up the largest age group at 30.73 percent, closely followed by those who were twenty-three to thirty years old, who made up 30.46 percent.

To help the researcher gauge the women's spiritual maturity as believers, they were asked to indicate how often they partake in the following Christian activities listed in table 1.

Table 1. Spiritual Maturity (Quantitative Survey)

	Never	A few times per year	Once or twice per month	Once or twice per week	Every day
I attend church	2.02 percent	6.79 percent	13.58 percent	75.23 percent	2.39 percent
I study the Bible (either alone, with a mentor, or in a small group)	2.39 percent	7.80 percent	13.30 percent	41.93 percent	34.59 percent
I pray to God	0.83 percent	1.38 percent	2.57 percent	17.98 percent	77.25 percent
I am in a Christian community where biblical topics are discussed	2.39 percent	5.60 percent	10.18 percent	49.45 percent	32.39 percent

These questions were used to gauge their spiritual maturity. Table 1 shows the spiritual maturity of the women who completed the survey by revealing that the majority are regular church attenders (75.23 percent attend church once or twice per week) and often study the Bible (41.93 percent study the Bible once or twice per week, and 34.59 percent, every day). The majority, 77.25 percent, of the women pray to God every day. Lastly, the participants are frequently in a Christian community where biblical topics are

Procedure and Research Method

discussed (49.45 percent, once or twice per week, and 32.39 percent, every day).

Lack of self-worth could point to a problem with sexual shame. To determine the participant's self-worth, the women were asked to grade how the statements on self-worth accurately reflected their life, from strongly disagree, disagree, indifferent, agree, to strongly agree. Here are the results:

Table 2. Self-Worth (Quantitative Survey)

	Strongly disagree	Disagree	Indifferent	Agree	Strongly agree
I feel good about who I am	2.48 percent	16.97 percent	13.94 percent	52.11 percent	14.50 percent
I feel worthwhile and valuable	2.20 percent	15.50 percent	14.50 percent	50.46 percent	17.34 percent
I am content in my relationship status	5.69 percent	17.06 percent	9.08 percent	29.17 percent	38.99 percent
I love myself	2.94 percent	13.39 percent	19.08 percent	50.64 percent	13.94 percent
I experience sexual shame	7.25 percent	21.28 percent	9.54 percent	47.71 percent	14.22 percent
I am free from sexual shame	13.03 percent	44.04 percent	11.38 percent	21.38 percent	10.18 percent

The majority of the participants marked "Agree" or "Strongly agree" for all of the categories above except for "I am free from sexual shame." The next chapter will look at the specific findings and correlations to the research to explain how women have experienced sexual shame and how they can find freedom.

Chapter 4

Research Findings

Introduction

CHAPTER 4 WILL LOOK at the research findings from the qualitative and quantitative surveys to discover how Christian women have experienced sexual shame and to answer the research question: "How do women find freedom from sexual shame?" Each qualitative-survey participant was given a fake name to keep stories consistent throughout the remaining chapters. The qualitative surveys quoted in this project will be included in the appendix. The survey responses in the appendices have not been edited for punctuation and grammar, except for obvious errors that hindered readability.

How Women Have Experienced Sexual Shame

Qualitative Survey

When asked, "Have you ever experienced sexual shame? Please share your story (open-ended)," all forty-four participants wrote out as much as they were willing of their story. The two most common themes among the stories were the following: seventeen (38.64 percent) wrote a story of experiencing sexual shame within sexual abuse or assault and thirteen (29.55 percent) shared stories of sexual shame surrounding pornography and masturbation.

Other stories of sexual shame included experiencing sexual shame from dating relationships, losing their virginity or feeling pressure to go further sexually than they wanted, same-sex attraction, affairs, and/or shame from having sexual desires.

When asked, "What are specific things you've heard ministers say about sexuality that brought more shame than good (open-ended)?" participants either said their church or home was silent on the topic or that they heard negative messages. Out of the forty-four participants, twelve (27.27 percent) stated that they never heard their pastors or families talk about sexuality or left the question blank (meaning they possibly never heard any messages about sexuality). This percentage is actually a lot lower than the 80 percent of clients Sellers mentioned that said their homes were silent or only talked negatively about sexuality.[1]

Some of the survey participants said that they got the impression that one cannot talk about sexuality at church or at home. Francesca,[2] a twenty-one-year-old woman, wrote that she struggled with porn addiction, masturbation, lust, and promiscuity yet never told her story to anyone because she had "no safe space to ask questions about sex."

One participant said that she only heard sex addressed for married people, but very rarely. More than half of the participants (59.09 percent), answered that they only heard negative things about sexuality from their ministers and pastors. One survey participant, Ashley,[3] a thirty-one-year-old woman, experienced sexual shame for not enjoying or desiring sex in her marriage. She believed that the complete lack of talking about sex/sexuality is what made sex seem so shameful for her. Her family never talked about sex in her home, or if it was mentioned, it was regarded as bad behavior. She said she was even rebuked for using the word "vagina." Placing shame onto someone for using the anatomical word for a body part is one example of a negative message about sex.

1. Sellers, *Sex*, 6, 105.
2. See Appendix C.
3. See Appendix D.

Other participants wrote examples of negative comments from pastors or ministers that were sexist or stereotypical. Brooklyn,[4] a twenty-eight-year-old woman, wrote about the gender stereotypes she heard in church and explained that she only ever heard messages about women needing to be gentle. Brooklyn said these messages confused her because "I wasn't very gentle. I was tomboyish and slightly loud and clumsy. I wasn't very womanlike according to the social norm and add that to my same-sex struggles—I was extra lost." Similar comments and findings can be found in Perry's research previously mentioned.[5]

Some of the participants wrote examples of shame from the way their pastor talked about different sexual struggles. Tanisha, who remained a virgin into her thirties, said that she was shamed into waiting.[6] Tanisha said a message she often heard at church was "You're going to hell if you have sex." She also said that any conversations about sexual desires were lumped into the "lust category," and she was told she needed "deliverance." This story relates to the research of Stringer, who said that historically, the church has stated that sexual desire is wrong.[7] Many of the participants in this research project have heard only negative messaging.

Grace, a twenty-nine-year-old woman, started looking at porn when she was eighteen years old.[8] She quickly developed a porn addiction, which led to a sex addiction. Her church included sexual issues such as lust and porn addiction in sermons; however, speakers emphasized these as "men's issues." Grace explained how it felt to be a woman hearing these messages: "It made me feel like a freak. The way they said men need to 'resist' their temptations while women need to be 'modest' and 'pure,' as if we have no temptations." Another participant, Jessica, a twenty-six-year-old woman, heard similar messages from her church and said, "Hearing that only the men struggle with pornography/masturbation/lust

4. See Appendix E.
5. Perry, *Addicted to Lust*, 90.
6. See Appendix F.
7. Stringer, *Unwanted*, 62.
8. See Appendix G.

communicated to me as a woman I was some form of alien, and needed to remain silent to keep myself safe."[9] Jessica grew up in a family that remained silent about sex and viewed conversations about it as taboo. Jessica wrote that she heard negative messages at church and heard no messages at home, "all of which added to the self-placed shame I already had from my thoughts and actions."

Other examples of unhelpful or inaccurate messages from ministers about sexuality were the following: "If you haven't experienced an orgasm, you haven't lived," "I know women don't struggle with sex," "Your future spouse will only want someone who is a virgin," "The female body is a stumbling block for all men and should be covered," and "Men can't control themselves." Wendy, a thirty-three-year-old woman, heard many of these messages and felt sexual shame as a preteen because of her developing female body.[10] Wendy would wear boy clothes and three sports bras at a time so that her chest was flat and no one would think she was too feminine. Wendy refused to show her collarbone when wearing a dress, because she saw her body as a stumbling block for men. Sadly, Wendy heard and believed that women were weak, and she said, "Growing up, I hated the fact that I was one. I was a part of the weaker sex. I was hurt that God made me into something so powerless."

The survey continued by asking the participants, "Please check off which of the following that you have struggled with." The women could select multiple from the list: promiscuity, lust, homosexuality, masturbation, and/or pornography. The data in figure 3 show the percentages of the participants who marked each issue.

---

9. See Appendix H.
10. See Appendix I.

Figure 3: Participants' Sexual Issues
(Qualitative Survey)

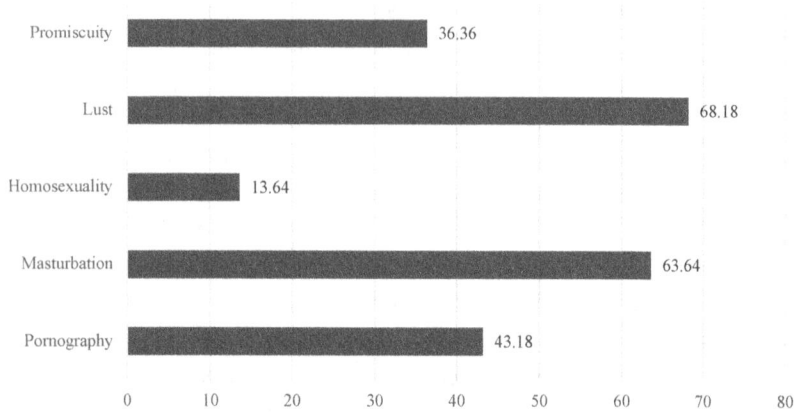

From highest to lowest percentages, the women selected that they struggle with lust, masturbation, pornography, promiscuity, and then homosexuality.

Lastly, when asked, "Share how your family talked about sex in the home. Were they comfortable with it? Were you shamed for sexual thoughts, questions, or behaviors in the home (open-ended)?" 70.45 percent said that sex was never talked about in the home.

Quantitative Survey

The women were asked in Q5, "How free do you feel from sexual shame?" on a scale from zero, not free at all, to one hundred, completely free. The average answer among the 1,090 participants was sixty-one. Figure 4 shows the results in numerical ranges.

Research Findings

Figure 4: How Free the Participants Feel (0–100) (Quantitative Survey)

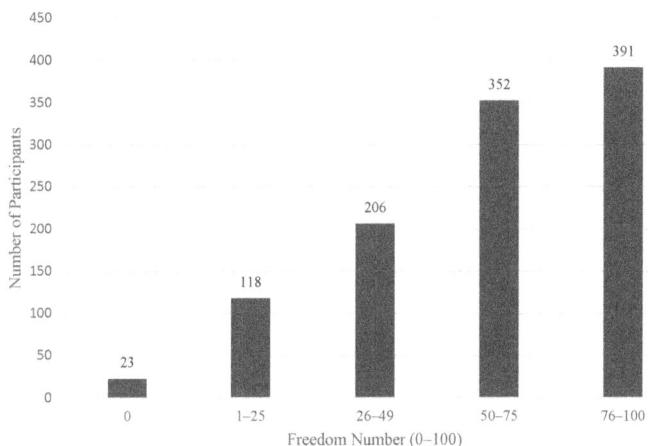

Figure 4 shows that 31.83 percent of the women answered 49 percent or less free, and the majority, 68.17 percent of the women, picked 50 percent or more free. Q5 was then correlated with the ages of the survey participants. See the figure below for correlation results.

Figure 5: How Free the Participants Feel (0–100) Correlated with Ages (Quantitative Survey)

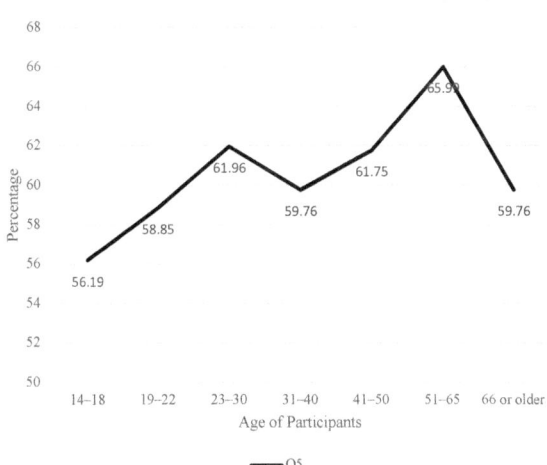

Figure 5 shows only a slight increase in the percentage of how free the participants feel from ages fourteen to thirty and then thirty-one to sixty-five; however, after thirty and sixty-five, there is a decrease in the percentages.

The ages of the participants were then correlated with Q4 to figure out if different ages were more or less likely to feel free from sexual shame or to experience sexual shame.

Figure 6: Comparing Ages with Sexual Shame (Quantitative Survey)

Age of Participants	I am free from sexual shame	I experience sexual shame
14–18	75	37.5
19–22	74.19	26.88
23–30	61.75	29.22
31–40	64.78	29.25
41–50	54.49	37.64
51–65	54.62	37.82
66 or older	58.82	35.29

The top line on the chart has a larger spread between the largest and smallest numbers compared to the bottom line on the chart. The top line has a 20.51 percent difference between those fourteen to eighteen years old to forty-one to fifty years old. The bottom line has only a 10.94 percent different between the freest age group, fifty-one to sixty-five years old, to the least free age group, nineteen to twenty-two years old.

The women were asked in Q6, "In the past, sexual shame has caused me to: (Please check all that apply)." The participants were able to select multiple answers, including the following: feel far from God, live a secret life (hide my activities from friends and family), avoid prayer, masturbate, doubt God's love for me, avoid reading Scripture, avoid authentic relationships, feel that God rejects me, feel that my sins cannot be forgiven by God, fear that God will not hear my prayers, doubt my salvation, turn to pornography, and leave my church or Christian community. The data in figure 7 shows the percentages of the participants who marked which issues from Q6.

Figure 7: Sexual Shame Caused Participants to . . . (Quantitative Survey)

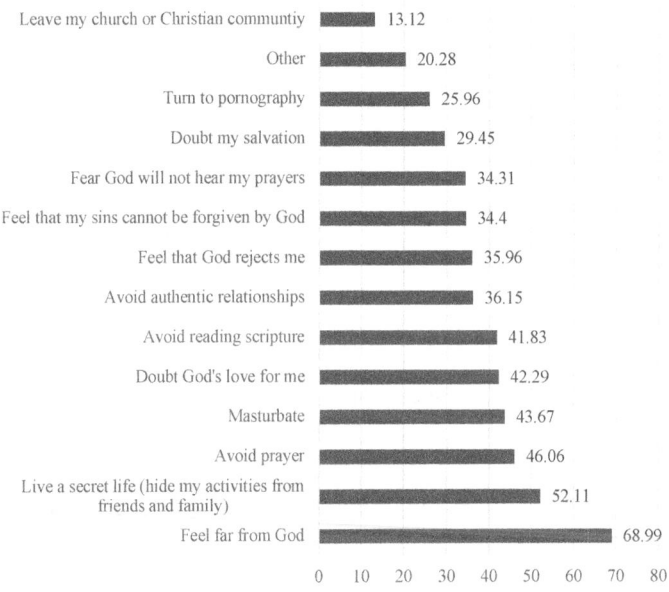

Figure 7 shows that for the majority of people, sexual shame has caused them to feel far from God (68.99 percent) and live a secret life (hiding their activities from friends and family) (52.11 percent). These findings are similar to those of Thompson, who previously stated that shame leads to isolation from others and God,[11] and to the research of Murray, Ciarrocchi, and Murray-Swank, who said the further one feels from God, the more shame they experience.[12]

11. Thompson, *Soul of Shame*, 113.
12. Murray et al., "Spirituality," 227.

The figure also shows that 25.96 percent of participants turned to pornography. When that percentage is broken down by age groups, 36.05 percent of those who are thirty or younger turned to porn, and 19.11 percent of those thirty-one or older. Thus, those thirty and under are almost twice as likely to turn to pornography than those thirty-one and older. This percentage is slightly less than the research that McDowell found in his research previously mentioned.[13]

In Q6, the participants were given the option to select "Other," and they could type in a response. Two hundred twenty-one participants typed in a response, and the researcher read each one. Participants said that sexual shame caused them to have an abortion, believe God hated them, try to numb the shame, believe the shame defined them, feel gross and less valuable as a woman, turn to legalism, and believe that they deserved to suffer. Common themes mentioned among the responses included the following: (1) destroyed relationships; (2) body shame; (3) broken church community; (4) anxiety and mental health problems. Each of these four main themes will be listed below with examples.

First of all, participants stated that sexual shame caused additional pain for relationships with friends, dating, and in marriage. One woman said she often felt "haunted by fear and shame about possibly 'flirting' or being 'seductive' when trying to make guy friends or even just hold eye contact during a conversation." Another woman felt such pressure that whomever she dated or even held hands with had to be "the one" to avoid creating more sexual shame. Many believed the lie that no Christian guy would ever want them because of their past or current struggles. Others attributed their singleness to being punished for their sin and felt like they were damaged goods.

Sexual shame hurt friendships with other women too. One participant said that sexual shame made her feel like her other Christian friends would be unable to relate or empathize, so she withdrew from her friendships. For others, codependent

---

13. McDowell, *Porn Phenomenon*, 58.

relationships became more prevalent. Others wrote that they constantly lied to their friends.

Sexual shame created problems in marriages as well. Participants said sexual shame caused problems surrounding sexual intimacy with their husbands. Common themes included the following: pulling away from their husbands and withdrawing; avoiding sexual pleasure and healthy sexual acts and encounters; doubting their husband's love; faking orgasms; lacking communication about sex; and feeling anxious about sex. One woman said she felt "guilty for having a sex drive," and another said she felt "like I'm broken and a disappointment to my spouse."

Secondly, many women said that sexual shame changed their view of their bodies and selves. One married woman said, "I'm never naked in front of anyone (husband of 21 years has NEVER seen me nude). I don't wear bathing suits, shorts or t-shirts." Other women commented that sexual shame caused them to disconnect from their bodies, wear ugly clothing, doubt their worth, and hate their bodies. One woman described the mental battle, specifically about her body: "I spiral into self-condemnation, body-image disgust, and shame about possibly being barren (because of Christian rhetoric about the worthiness of child-bearing women)."

Next, for some participants, sexual shame caused problems in their church community. One woman wrote that she "avoided reporting sexual assault and rape out of fear of shame in the eyes of my church." Another wrote that she was "angry with the Christian community for blaming me for being a survivor of abuse by a pastor on their campus." Others felt ostracized from their Christian community or avoided their Christian communities completely. One participant wrote, "I'm gay; I didn't go to sleep as a teen because I thought I'd die in my sleep and go to hell. I left 'the church' and started getting better after that." Others have rejected the Creator because they believed God made them "too sexual" but they were not allowed to be a sexual being.

Lastly, for many, sexual shame led to anxiety issues. The participants commented that they were mad at themselves and repulsed by who they were as women, and thus they turned to self-harm, depression, suicidal thoughts, panic attacks, and anxiety. One woman wrote, "I cry in private and smile in public." The comments made by the participants align with the conclusions of May and Alix.[14]

The next question, Q7, asks, "What sexual acts made/makes me experience sexual shame: (Please check all that apply)." Figure 8 shows the results from Q7.

Figure 8: What Sexual Acts Made/Make Participants Experience Sexual Shame (Quantitative Survey)

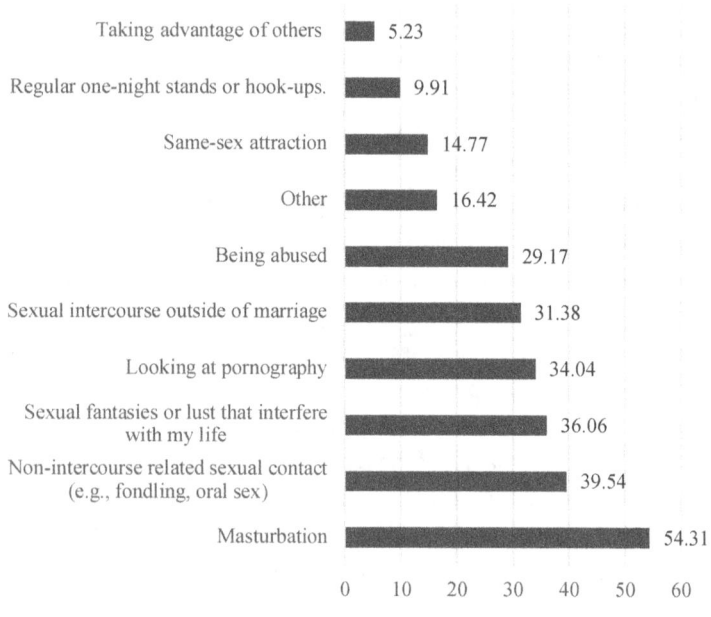

The chart above shows the percentages of people who experienced sexual shame after the sexual acts listed. The top answer from Q7 is masturbation (54.31 percent). The next four responses are in the 30 percent category: nonintercourse-related sexual contact (e.g., fondling, oral sex), sexual fantasies or lust that interfere with life, looking at pornography, and sexual intercourse outside of

---

14. May, *Addiction and Grace*, 55; Alix et al., "Self-Blame," 1–16.

marriage. Figure 8 does not show the percentage of participants who did each sexual act, but rather what percentage experienced shame about that act. A similar question was asked to the participants of the qualitative survey (see figure 3) and had similar responses. Masturbation and lust were both in the top three most selected responses for both surveys.

Similar to Q6, the participants were given the option to select "Other," and they could type in a response. One hundred seventy-nine participants typed in a response, and the researcher read each response to look for common themes. Common sexual acts written in were sexting, reading erotica, and sexual childhood pretend play with friends. There were common themes mentioned among the responses, including sexual acts done with significant others, sexual acts done by others, sexual acts in marriage, and sexual shame from lack of sexual acts or messages about sex because of the purity-culture narrative. Each of these four main themes will be listed below with examples.

First, one common theme mentioned was that of sexual acts done with significant others in dating relationships. Some of the participants wrote: "Going 'too far' before marriage (not including intercourse but other things)," "Fooling around before marriage," "Giving in to the pressure," "Non-sexual but romantic cuddling, tickling, holding . . . with someone who I was not officially in a relationship with."

Participants wrote in sexual acts done by others. Some of the frequent answers included actions done by the husband: affair or cheating, emotional affair, sleeping with prostitutes, or pornography. One woman stated her painful experience in finding out her husband's secret: "My husband came out last year with a sexual/porn addiction. I was a virgin when we got married, he was not, so my shame comes from not being what he expects." Other responses were examples of sexual abuse in marriage. One wife wrote about her husband: "We had to have sex at least every other day. At times he would get angry when I would fall asleep, throw cold water on me, and do things to keep me awake."

Next, examples of sexual shame came from sexual acts in marriage, mostly surrounding a woman's sexual desire—women either experienced sexual shame for having no sexual desire or for having a libido higher than that of their husband. For many participants, sexual shame prevented them from enjoying sex at all or communicating with their husband about their needs and desires. For one woman, she felt sexual shame when "wearing items (clothes or lingerie) that made me feel confident, but would be seen as too sexually tempting." Another participant wrote, "It was years before I was able to orgasm, but it took so much time and effort that I didn't enjoy it." Many participants said that they, too, experienced sexual shame from being unable to orgasm. One woman, who was married for over thirty-seven years, said that she never enjoyed sex, which resulted in her avoiding it. Women commonly included pain in sex as a sexual experience that made them feel sexual shame.

Lastly, participants mentioned that their lack of sexual acts or messages about sex caused sexual shame because of the narratives from the purity culture. One woman said that she was told to abstain from sex and to fear sex because "it was bad." Then, when she got married at thirty-seven years old, it took her three years to "feel okay about it." Many women mentioned a belief that sex was immoral or that sexual pleasure displeased God. One participant wrote that she was "made to feel my sexuality and desire was unfeminine and ungodly." Other participants mentioned messages from their church that caused sexual shame: "the Billy Graham Rule," "being rejected from church leadership due to my female body," "nonsexual touch that was sexualized by my Christian culture," and "fundamentalism or distorted teachings that emphasize works, especially sexual purity or more accurately perfection." Another woman wrote that as she grew up, she was told that "sexuality was something to be downplayed and hidden." Finally, a single woman wrote the way these messages made her feel about her sexuality:

> I am a virgin. I grew up in the height of the purity-culture movement and adhered to its teachings like a "good Christian girl" should. I'm 34 and have never dated, much less had sex outside of marriage. However, I feel shame

Research Findings

at being so inexperienced in my mid 30s. Purity-culture teachings caused me to internalize the belief that I am unworthy of being in a healthy relationship, unlovable, and that my body is something to be hidden and ashamed of.

Then, the participants were asked in Q8, "What other social factors made/make me experience sexual shame? (Please check all that apply.)" The percentages of the participants that selected each answer are shown in figure 9.

Figure 9: What Social Factors Made/Make Participants Experience Sexual Shame (Quantitative Survey)

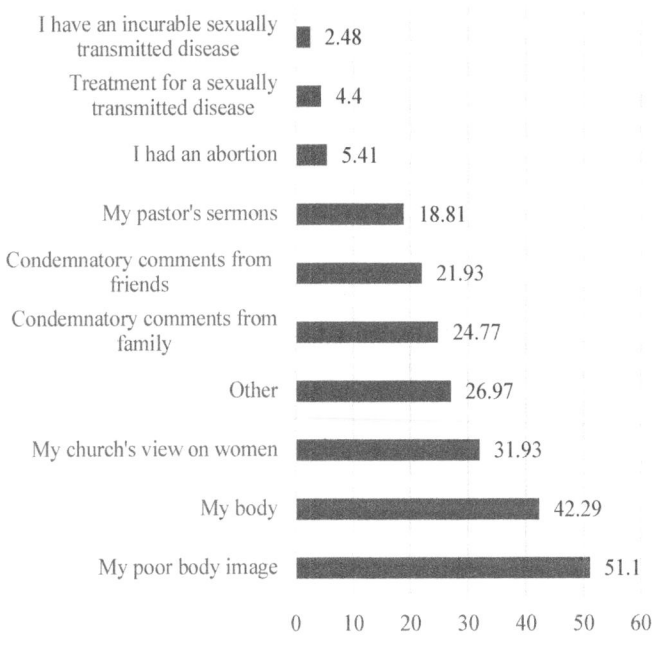

Figure 9 shows that the top two answers of what social factors made/make participants experience sexual shame were "My poor body image" and "My body." It makes sense that those who have poor body image experience more sexual shame. This data is supported by Brown's study on women and shame previously mentioned.[15]

15. Brown, "Shame Resilience Theory," 43–52.

A correlation exists between a participant's freedom-from-shame percentage and their level of self-esteem. For example, those who said they "Agree" or "Strongly agree" to "I feel good about who I am" (726 participants) had an average freedom-from-shame number of 68.96 percent, versus those who said they "Disagree" or "Strongly disagree" (212 participants); these had an average of 43.33 percent. Similarly, those who said they "Agree" or "Strongly agree" to "I feel worthwhile and valuable" (739 participants) had an average freedom-from-shame number of 68.72 percent, versus those who said they "Disagree" or "Strongly disagree" (193 participants), who had an average of 43.16 percent. Thus, the better one felt about herself, her body, and her worth, the freer she felt from sexual shame.

In figure 9, 294 people filled in a response for "Other." Popular themes mentioned in those responses included the following: relationship status (i.e., shame from being single), relationship issues (i.e., a spouse cheating on them or getting caught using porn), believing lies about self, anxiety, the purity movement, and rape-culture myths.

Quantitative Survey Correlations with "I Experience Sexual Shame"

Out of the 1,090 responses, 675 answered that they either "Agree" or "Strongly agree" to "I experience sexual shame" in Q4. To figure out what sexual shame causes, the researcher correlated these 675 participants with popular choices from Q6 ("In the past, sexual shame has caused me to do the following"). Table 3 shows the correlation between Q4 (those who "Agree" or "Strongly agree" with "I experience sexual shame") and Q6 (those who marked off one of the categories).

In tables 3, 4, and 5, the right column shows the percentages of the correlated participants. The first number is the number of people within that group who chose the correlating response, while the second number is the number of people who "Agree" or "Strongly agree" that they experience sexual shame.

Research Findings

Table 3. Q4 and Q6 Correlations (Quantitative Survey)

Feel far from God	525/675 (77.78 percent)
Doubt God's love for me	355/675 (52.59 percent)
Feel that God rejects me	304/675 (45.04 percent)
Avoid authentic friendships	299/675 (44.30 percent)
Live a secret life; hide my activities from friends and family	402/675 (59.56 percent)
Leave my church	108/675 (16.00 percent)
Feel that my sins cannot be forgiven by God	282/675 (41.78 percent)

The largest correlation is with those who selected "Feel far from God," as 77.78 percent of participants who experience sexual shame feel far from God. Similar to the research of Murray, Ciarrocchi, and Murray-Swank,[16] this data shows that those who feel close to God are on average 12.5 percent freer than those who feel far from God.

The second-largest correlation is with those who selected "Live a secret life; hide my activities from friends and family." More than half of the participants, 59.56 percent, experience sexual shame that causes them to hide their lives from their loved ones. Also, 52.59 percent of the women doubt God's love, which is a similar finding to the work of Ferree, who stated that women who remain in sexual sin frequently doubt God's love.[17]

The researcher then took those same 675 people who answered that they either "Agree" or "Strongly agree" to "I experience sexual shame" in Q4 and correlated it to Q7, "What sexual acts

---

16. Murray et al., "Spirituality," 227.

17. Ferree, *No Stones*, 30–31.

made/make me experience sexual shame?" Those results are in table 4.

Table 4. Q4 and Q7 Correlations (Quantitative Survey)

Looking at pornography	270/675 (40.00 percent)
Being abused	247/675 (36.59 percent)
Masturbation	416/675 (61.63 percent)
Sexual fantasies or lust that interfere with my life	284/675 (42.07 percent)

Again, the researcher took those same 675 people who answered that they either "Agree" or "Strongly agree" to "I experience sexual shame" in Q4 and correlated it to Q8, "What other factors made/make me experience sexual shame? (Please check all that apply.)" Those results are in table 5.

Table 5. Q4 and Q8 Correlations (Quantitative Survey)

Poor body image	404/675 (59.85 percent)
My body	344/675 (50.96 percent)
My church's view of women	253/675 (37.48 percent)

Similar to the results from Q8, the highest two answers are "Poor body image" and "My body." When a woman experiences sexual shame from "Poor body image," this refers to the mental perception of her body, versus sexual shame from "My body," which is the actual or objective physical body. The researcher also correlated those who selected that "My church's view of women" or "My pastor's sermons" caused sexual shame (Q8) with those who choose

Research Findings

"Leave my church or Christian community" (Q6) to see if the shame from the church and pastor led to participants leaving their church. The survey showed that 21.55 percent of women who experienced sexual shame from their church's view of women ended up leaving their church or Christian community. The correlation also showed that 24.39 percent of women who experienced sexual shame from their pastor's sermons also left the church or Christian community.

How Women Experienced Freedom from Sexual Shame

Now the researcher will explore how survey participants experienced freedom from sexual shame.

Figure 10 displays the percentages from Q9, "What non-biblical sources free me from my sexual shame? (Please check all that apply.)," and figure 11 will display the percentages from Q10, "What biblical sources or spiritual actions free me from my sexual shame? (Please check all that apply.)," both from the quantitative survey. Table 6 correlates the participants' ages from the quantitative survey with their responses to specific chosen answers from Q9 and Q10 to see if participants are more likely to find freedom from sexual shame at different ages. Figure 12 shows the estimated percentages from the open-ended question "What helped you find freedom from sexual shame?" from the qualitative survey.

Figure 10: Non-biblical Sources that Provide Freedom from Sexual Shame (Quantitative Survey)

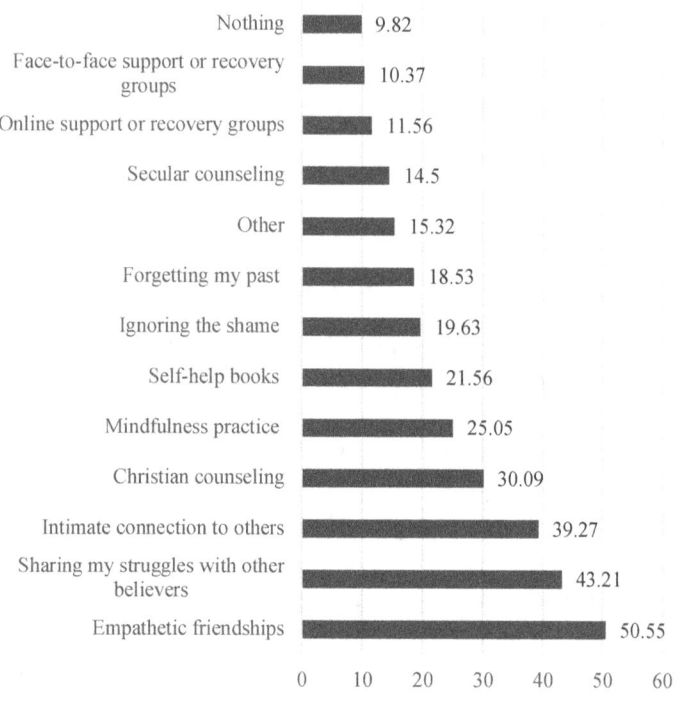

Figure 10 reveals that the top three non-biblical sources that provide freedom from sexual shame are as follows: "Empathetic friendships," "Sharing my struggles with other believers," and "Intimate connection to others."

In the survey, 167 participants answered "Other." The researcher read all of the "Other" comments and discovered a source that will be addressed in chapter 5. Many participants talked about how a loving husband helped them find freedom from sexual shame.

Research Findings

Figure 11: Biblical Sources or Spiritual Actions That Provide Freedom from Sexual Shame (Quantitative Survey)

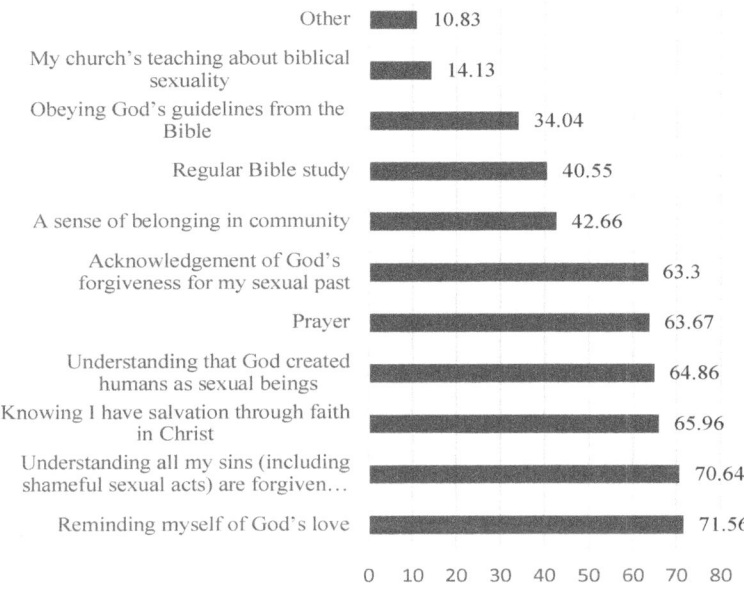

Figure 11 states that the most picked answer for a biblical source or spiritual action that provides freedom from sexual shame is "Reminding myself of God's love," and a close second is "Understanding all my sins (including shameful sexual acts) are forgiven through Christ's death." The least picked answer, "Other," was selected by 118 people, and again, many participants commented on the healing power of a loving and supportive husband. One participant said, "My husband's understanding of sex in marriage and his attentiveness to our marriage's sexual health [provides freedom]." Another said, "Praying with my husband when I struggle." Other common responses included experiencing empathy and Christian blogs and books on sexuality.

Table 6: Age Correlations with How Participants Experience Freedom from Sexual Shame (Quantitative Survey)
(italics = the highest in each row)

	14–18 years old	19–22 years old	23–30 years old	31–40 years old	41–50 years old	51–65 years old	66 and older
Sharing my struggles with other believers	6/16 (37.5 percent)	49/93 (*52.69 percent*)	168/332 (50.60 percent)	150/335 (44.78 percent)	62/178 (34.83 percent)	32/119 (26.89 percent)	3/17 (17.65 percent)
Intimate connections to others	6/16 (37.5 percent)	44/93 (*47.31 percent*)	147/332 (44.28 percent)	133/335 (39.70 percent)	58/178 (32.58 percent)	34/119 (28.57 percent)	6/17 (35.29 percent)
Empathetic friendships	4/16 (25 percent)	51/93 (54.84 percent)	195/332 (*58.73 percent*)	181/335 (54.03 percent)	70/178 (39.33 percent)	44/119 (36.97 percent)	6/17 (35.29 percent)
Christian counseling, online support or recovery groups, or face-to-face support or recovery groups	6/16 (37.5 percent)	37/93 (39.78 percent)	145/332 (43.67 percent)	151/335 (*45.07 percent*)	53/178 (29.78 percent)	48/119 (40.34 percent)	7/17 (41.18 percent)
Reminding myself of God's love	15/16 (*93.75 percent*)	74/93 (79.57 percent)	248/332 (74.70 percent)	228/335 (68.06 percent)	114/178 (64.04 percent)	88/119 (73.95 percent)	15/17 (88.24 percent)
Acknowledgement of God's forgiveness for my sexual past	12/16 (*75 percent*)	63/93 (67.74 percent)	210/332 (63.25 percent)	205/335 (61.19 percent)	106/178 (59.55 percent)	85/119 (71.43 percent)	9/17 (52.94 percent)

Research Findings

	14–18 years old	19–22 years old	23–30 years old	31–40 years old	41–50 years old	51–65 years old	66 and older
Understanding that God created humans as sexual beings	11/16 (68.75 percent)	62/93 (66.67 percent)	234/332 (*70.49 percent*)	225/335 (67.16 percent)	95/178 (53.37 percent)	70/119 (58.82 percent)	9/17 (52.94 percent)
Understanding all my sins (including shameful sexual acts) are forgiven through Christ's death	12/16 (75 percent)	70/93 (*75.27 percent*)	247/332 (74.40 percent)	226/335 (67.46 percent)	123/178 (69.10 percent)	81/119 (68.07 percent)	10/17 (58.82 percent)
A sense of belonging in community	10/16 (*62.5 percent*)	49/93 (52.69 percent)	158/332 (47.59 percent)	147/335 (43.88 percent)	57/178 (32.02 percent)	38/119 (31.93 percent)	6/17 (35.29 percent)
My church's teaching about biblical sexuality	5/16 (*31.25 percent*)	13/93 (13.98 percent)	60/332 (18.07 percent)	49/335 (14.63 percent)	17/178 (9.55 percent)	9/119 (7.56 percent)	1/17 (5.88 percent)

Table 6 correlates the participants' ages from the quantitative survey with their responses to specific chosen answers from Q9 and Q10 to see if people in different age ranges are more likely to find freedom from sexual shame in different ways than participants of other ages. For each answer or row, the highest percentage was italicized, and the highest answer in the column of options, which was "Reminding myself of God's love," was also italicized.

Figure 12 shows the estimated percentages from the open-ended question from the qualitative-survey question "What helped you find freedom from sexual shame?" Because the question was open-ended, the researcher read through each response and grouped the answers by category and theme. The results are provided in Figure 12.

Figure 12: Sources That Provide Freedom from Sexual Shame (Qualitative Survey)

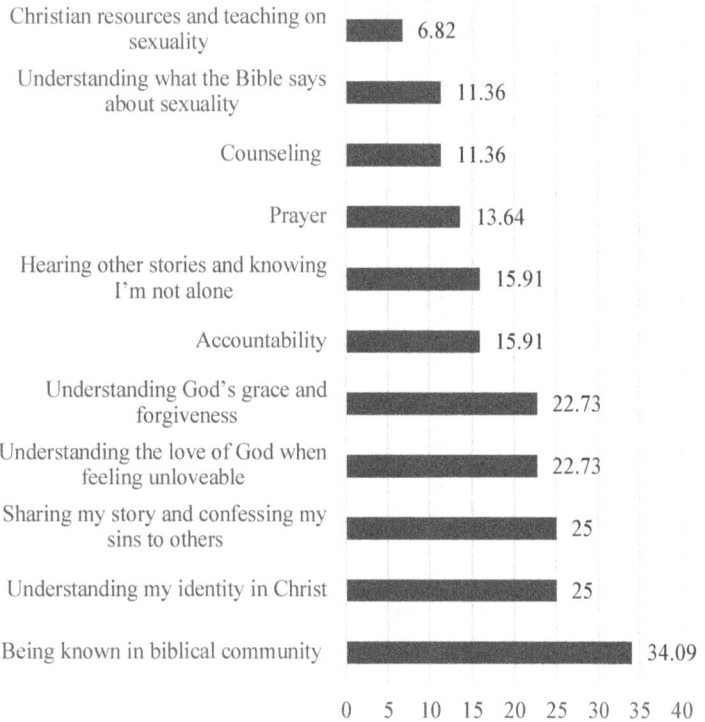

The number-one theme from responses in the open-ended question was "Being known in biblical community." There was a tie for the second-highest theme: "Understanding my identity in Christ" and "Sharing my story and confessing my sins to others." These results are similar to Q9 and Q10 from the quantitative survey.

The next section will look at the results from the two surveys and how they directly apply to the three hypotheses.

Research Findings

Hypothesis 1

Hypothesis 1 states, "Christian women will identify understanding the love and grace of God as a key factor in finding freedom from sexual shame."

As Christian women grow in understanding the love and grace of God, they will also grow in understanding their freedom in Christ. Knowing ones' identity in Jesus frees her from shame—this was true for Holly.[18] Holly is a Christian woman who has struggled with pornography, masturbation, and homosexuality. Holly experienced sexual shame from a few different situations: she was raised in a non-Christian home where there were jokes about being gay, she was molested as a young teen by a family member, and she had an affair with a lesbian woman. Holly said that she is only just now finding freedom as a sixty-nine-year-old woman by going to a Christian therapist. For Holly, it was not just going to therapy that brought her freedom; it was the fact that her therapist explained to her the freedom Christ offers and the grace that is available in knowing God.

Similar to Holly, Anna, a forty-two-year-old woman, also struggled with sexual shame surrounding same-sex relationships, pornography, and masturbation.[19] She also experienced sexual abuse as a child. When asked, "What helped you find freedom from sexual shame?" she responded, "Knowing that God forgives me and loves me." Understanding God's forgiveness is key to finding freedom from sexual shame. Holly and Anna's stories are similar to the 161 women who selected "same-sex attraction" as something that causes sexual shame. Fifty-nine percent of those who experienced sexual shame from same-sex attraction also doubt God's love. This finding is similar to that of Yuan.[20] Interestingly, of these same 161 women who struggle with same-sex attraction, 80.75 percent live a life they keep secret from family and friends and most likely have not shared their struggle with loved ones.

18. See Appendix J.
19. See Appendix K.
20. Yuan, *Holy Sexuality*, 72.

Andrea,[21] a thirty-seven-year-old woman, chose to abort her baby, and the shame she experienced led to her living a life of continued sexual sin. Andrea said that she believed that God could never love or forgive her because of her actions, which led to her walking away from God for years. When asked what brought her freedom, she said that it was only because she began to understand God's forgiveness and assurance.

Bailey[22] was sexually abused as a child. When she was only nine years old, her cousin began molesting her, and it continued for four years. Now a thirty-five-year-old woman, Bailey said that the only way she was able to find freedom was because of Christ. She said, "He showed me how he sees me and that he washed the shame away." Finding freedom in Christ was also the experience of a participant of the quantitative survey. For Q10, a woman who experienced sexual abuse commented, "Remembering that my shame is caused by someone else's sin, not my own, and understanding that Jesus died not only for my sins, but also the sins that were committed against me. He took the burden of what I did wrong, but also takes the burden of the wrongs others put on me." Understanding the cross brought her healing through Christ.

Adaobi, a single twenty-one-year-old woman, also experienced the healing power of Christ.[23] Adaobi lives in Nigeria and stated that when she was growing up, her family talked about sex only as a warning against unwanted pregnancies. She was told that if she ever became pregnant, she would be thrown out of her house. Because her family and church never created a safe place for her to talk about sexuality, she kept her struggles with pornography, masturbation, and lust a secret. The condemnatory comments from her family resulted in intense sexual shame that led to suicidal ideation. When asked what brought her freedom, she said:

> Christ. I gave my life to him. I poured everything out to him. He saved me, took everything away including the shame I was walking around with. Before, I was a living

21. See Appendix L.
22. See Appendix M.
23. See Appendix N.

dead. But Christ came and took all of it away. He healed my poor and fragile heart. He healed my misery. He gave me hope and grace, one I wasn't worthy of. My life is nothing without him.

Zendaya, a forty-six-year-old woman, also credits Christ for her freedom from shame.[24] As an eleven-year-old girl, she was molested by her cousin. This traumatic event, followed by the constant verbal abuse from her father, who eventually left her family, resulted in sexual shame. Zendaya recounted stories of her father looking at pornography and comparing the women in the porn to her body, saying she needed to lose weight. Because of her body and sexual shame, Zendaya fell into a pattern of promiscuity in high school as a means of seeking love, only to be greatly disappointed. The turning point in her story happened when she became a Christian in college. Over time, she began to understand Christ's love for her and his atoning work on her behalf. Zendaya wrote in the survey, "I was washed clean and given new life. New life in Christ and a new life free from shame." Understanding her new identity in Christ helped free her from sexual shame.

Jennifer, a thirty-seven-year-old woman, experienced sexual shame from lust and promiscuity.[25] She ultimately found freedom from understanding God's grace. Jennifer wrote:

> The Holy Spirit revealed to me that there was nothing I could do to be considered "good enough." That Jesus gave me his righteousness in exchange for my sin. I needed to let God love me, and I needed to receive his love. When my eyes were opened to God's infinite, never ending love no matter the things I've done, my perspective was changed. I didn't allow the enemy to whisper lies into my ear any longer.

Understanding the love of God through Jesus was the key for Jennifer to find freedom from sexual shame. The stories in this section align with the results from Q10 in the quantitative survey.

---

24. See Appendix O.
25. See Appendix P.

Q10 asked, "What biblical sources or spiritual actions free me from my sexual shame?" See figure 11 for the complete data, but the answers that relate to hypothesis 1 are as follows:

- 71.56 percent, reminding myself of God's love
- 70.64 percent, understanding all my sins (including shameful sexual acts) are forgiven through Christ's death
- 65.96 percent, knowing I have salvation through faith in Christ
- 63.67 percent, prayer
- 63.30 percent, acknowledgement of God's forgiveness for my sexual past.

All of the answers above show the importance of either understanding theology or growing a relationship with God to find freedom from sexual shame. One way to learn theology and get to know God is through studying the Bible. In the quantitative survey, Q3 asked participants to indicate how often they studied the Bible. The researcher divided the participants into their frequency categories and found the average for their answer to Q5, "How free do you feel from sexual shame?" Figure 13 on the next page shows that as the time spent reading the Bible increased, so did the level of freedom the participant felt from sexual shame.

Figure 13: Time Spent Studying the Bible Correlated to Freedom from Sexual Shame (Quantitative Survey)

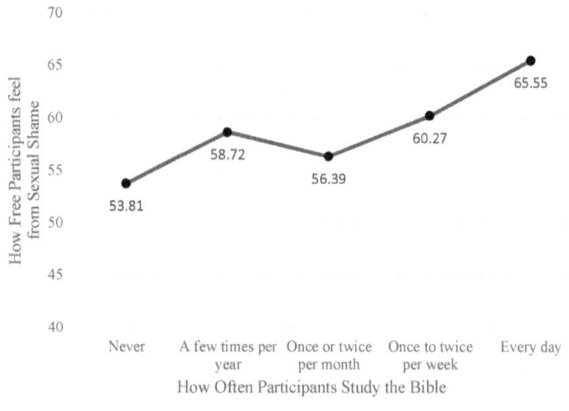

Research Findings

In figure 13, one can see an 11.74 percent increase in freedom from sexual shame for those who study the Bible every day from those who never study the Bible.

Hypothesis 2

Hypothesis 2 states, "Christian women will identify being known in biblical community as a key factor in finding freedom from sexual shame."

Many of the survey responders said that being known in biblical community was key to helping them find freedom from sexual shame. In the quantitative survey, 42.66 percent of participants stated they needed to feel a sense of belonging in community to help them find freedom. This was true for Aubrey, a thirty-one-year-old woman who was date-raped and then turned to promiscuity because of her sexual shame.[26] Her sexual choices created more sexual shame and led her to feel far from God. When asked how she found freedom, she said, "Turning to God and finding a Christ-centered-community that could help me get over my shame and guilt has helped more than anything." Being a part of a Christ-centered community gave her a place where she felt like she belonged.

To discover if biblical community, as previously defined, is a key to finding freedom, Q3 asked participants to indicate how often they attend church and are in Christian community. The researcher divided the participants into their frequency categories and found the average for their answer to Q5, "How free do you feel from sexual shame?" Figures 14 and 15 show that the more a participant attends church or is a part of a Christian community, the freer the participant feels from sexual shame.

In figure 14, one can see a 14.2 percent increase in freedom from sexual shame for those who attend church every day or once or twice per week from those who never attend church. Similarly, in figure 15, there is also an increase, but to a smaller degree. There

---

26. See Appendix Q.

is a 5.83 percent increase in freedom from sexual shame for those who are in Christian community every day or once or twice per week from those who never or only a few times per year are in Christian community.

Figure 14: Church Attendance Correlated to Freedom from Sexual Shame (Quantitative Survey)

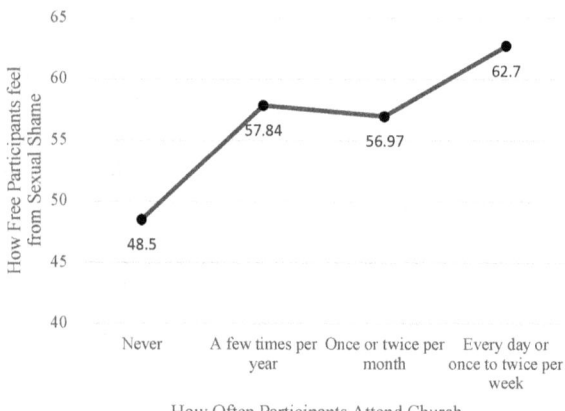

Figure 15: Christian-Community Involvement Correlated to Freedom from Sexual Shame (Quantitative Survey)

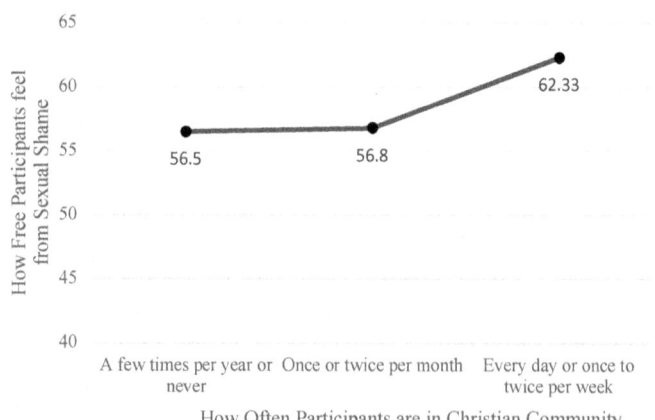

Research Findings

In addition to being found through church attendance, biblical community is also found through mentors and discipleship. Stacy, a twenty-eight-year-old woman, found freedom from sexual shame through the vulnerability of a mentor.[27] Before finding her mentor, Stacy struggled alone:

> Growing up it was never safe to ask my parents (or anyone I knew) questions about sex. It would always turn into "I had done something wrong." I grew up feeling bad about my sexuality and soon turned to pornography and masturbation in secret because I couldn't open up to anyone about how I was struggling. I didn't know another woman who struggled with these things or even had sexual desire of her own. I thought I was the only one! Every book or sermon on the subject only mentioned male desire.

Stacy also said that when she would ask her parents questions about sex, she got in trouble. Eventually, she stopped asking questions and began to believe that sex was bad and should not be talked about. She also believed that God did not care about her sexuality. When asked, "What helped you find freedom from sexual shame?" Stacy wrote this:

> It wasn't until a mentor led with vulnerability and shared about her own struggles that I felt safe to share my own sin. She pointed me to the gospel and how God knew the whole time and still sent Jesus to make a way for me to have relationship with him. This gave me the strength to keep being vulnerable with that mentor and pursue accountability and healing of those deeper issues. Over time I felt safe enough and secure in God to share my stories with others and help them start their recovery journey.

Stacy's experience is similar to others. Brandi, a thirty-four-year-old woman, struggled with reading erotica and masturbation.[28] When asked how she found freedom, she wrote, "Finding

27. See Appendix R.
28. See Appendix S.

an accountability partner and confessing my sins. This helped me to repent and finally grab hold of the grace and forgiveness that Christ freely offers." Accountability was key for Carrie, too.[29] A thirty-six-year-old woman, Carrie struggled with pornography and masturbation. Early in her struggle, her Bible-study leader brought up pornography and offered to be an accountability partner for anyone struggling. Carrie said that she met with her and confessed her struggle, because "she was a safe person." Having a safe person to talk with is key to finding freedom. Francesca, who was mentioned earlier and who said she had "no safe space to ask questions about sex," stated she found freedom by "being able to talk to other women about things I am usually ashamed to talk about."[30] Having safe and empathetic people to whom one can tell one's painful story was also found in the quantitative survey. Q9 asked, "What non-biblical sources free me from my sexual shame?" From the survey, 50.55 percent of participants said, "Empathetic friendships," 43.21 percent said, "Sharing my struggles with other believers," and 39.27 percent said, "Intimate connection to others"—all of which are represented in Stacy's and Francesca's stories. Previous research has also shown that the best treatment for sexual shame is bonding through intimate connection with others.[31]

Brooklyn, who was previously mentioned as a woman who struggled with sexual shame because of gender stereotypes, found freedom through sharing her story with safe people and realizing she was not alone in her struggle.[32] When asked what brought her freedom, she wrote this:

> Verbally speaking about my shame was the first step in helping me find freedom. Every time I shared to someone about my stories and struggles, I felt less alone. This eventually helped me speak to God more honestly about my shame and also pushed me to actually obey the

29. See Appendix T.
30. See Appendix C.
31. Adams and Robinson, "Shame Reduction," 23.
32. See Appendix E.

Research Findings

Scriptures and intently battle with the thoughts in my mind.

Once Brooklyn was able to find freedom from her sexual shame through the power of sharing her story and no longer feeling alone, then she was able to turn to God and obey him with her sexuality. Jackie, a twenty-seven-year-old woman who was addicted to masturbation, also found freedom from sharing her story and no longer felt alone.[33] She first heard someone confess their struggle and realized that person was not defined by it. After knowing that the woman could relate to her struggle of dealing with sexual brokenness, Jackie was encouraged to tell her story too. Jackie stated, "Knowing there was a point of relating helped me not feel alone and was what I needed to be vulnerable."

Grace, previously mentioned, found freedom through confession, accountability, and a support group.[34] To her surprise, after confessing her pornography addiction to her pastor, she was met with grace and compassion. She learned that her pastor also struggled with pornography when he was younger. Her pastor then encouraged her to talk with a woman at their church, who became her accountability partner. Grace said that having someone to talk to and be with on her recovery journey was amazing. She also found freedom by joining a support group for women who suffer from love and sex addiction.

Juliana, a twenty-five-year-old woman, struggled with masturbation but kept it a secret.[35] Explaining her fear, she wrote, "I think there is so much stigma around women and sexual sin. I felt that I would be judged or looked down upon if I shared." Her comment reflects the research of Ferree, who mentioned the inhibiting power of fear, which prevents healing.[36] In order for Juliana to find freedom from sexual shame, her fear had to be dismantled, and

---

33. See Appendix U.
34. See Appendix G.
35. See Appendix V.
36. Ferree, *No Stones*, 29–30.

thankfully, it was. Juliana stated what helped her eventually find freedom from sexual shame:

> Hearing other women's similar stories showed me that I was not alone and that my struggles with sexual sin do not disqualify me as a Christian. I am so thankful to know that I am not alone, and I am not unlovable or unworthy. If I had not heard other women's stories, I may not have ever a) confronted my struggles head on or b) had the courage and the confidence in Christ to share my struggles.

Being known in community can look different for everyone. For some, community may include support groups or counseling. Victoria, a forty-seven-year-old woman, grew up in an emotionally abusive home and was sexually harassed since age eleven.[37] She found freedom from her sexual shame from the community of Celebrate Recovery groups. She wrote, "Listening to other women's stories and sharing the pain with others is remarkably healing." Victoria's story aligns with results from Q9 in the quantitative survey: "What non-biblical sources free me from my sexual shame?" The survey showed that 11.56 percent of participants chose online support or recovery groups and 10.37 percent chose face-to-face support or recovery groups.

For Wendy, counseling helped her find freedom from sexual shame.[38] She said that going to counseling helped her to work on her identity issues and to find friendships to support her. Like Wendy, participants' responses to Q9 in the quantitative survey, "What non-biblical sources free me from my sexual shame?" included the following: 30.09 percent, Christian counseling, and 14.50 percent, secular counseling.

For most women, a combination of different factors needs to happen for them to begin finding freedom. Jessica[39] found freedom from her sexual shame by hearing other women talk openly about sexuality, learning about the neurological patterns for

37. See Appendix W.
38. See Appendix I.
39. See Appendix H.

addiction, and reading the Bible to learn what Scripture says about sex and sexuality.

The last hypothesis will explore how women find freedom through a biblical teaching of sexuality.

Hypothesis 3

Hypothesis 3 states, "Christian women will identify learning a biblical teaching of sexuality as a key factor in finding freedom from sexual shame."

When asked if they experienced freedom from "My church's teaching about biblical sexuality," only 14.13 percent selected that response when looking at all 1,090 quantitative participants. Interestingly, this percentage greatly varies depending on the age range. (See table 6 for all the percentages for each age range.) Not surprisingly, the age ranges that have the lowest percentages of participants who chose "My church's teaching about biblical sexuality" are those age sixty-six and older, followed by those fifty-one to sixty-five years old, and then those forty-one to fifty years old. Those fourteen to eighteen years old are more than three times more likely to find freedom from their church's teaching on biblical sexuality than those forty-one and older.

When asked Q10, "What biblical sources or spiritual actions free me from my sexual shame?" 64.86 percent of participants selected understanding that God created humans as sexual beings, which is the fourth-highest answer in Q10.

One participant found freedom when she realized that her church's teaching on sexuality did not align with God's word. In the "Other" category of Q9, she wrote, "Recognizing that the way the church and people view sex and how God intended sex are different"—thus, she wrote about the importance of reading God's word for herself to learn what the Bible does say about sexuality. Similarly, Kayla, a twenty-nine-year-old woman, experienced sexual shame because she did not know that God created sexual desire.[40] She grew up in a family that was embarrassed talking about sexuality, and she was sometimes shamed for talking about it. Kayla recounted, "I remember being ashamed of my first crush because I didn't want others to know that I had sexual desires." As she got older, she read Christian books and blogs that made her realize how God created sex and that it was a good thing for a married man and woman. Kayla said that these Christian resources and the Bible, especially King Solomon's poems, helped her understand biblical sexuality and that God places a high value on sex and sexuality.

Conclusion

In conclusion, the three hypotheses accurately predicted the findings from the two surveys and the literary review included in chapter 2. The first and second hypotheses had more quantitative and qualitative data to support their claims than the third hypothesis. The final chapter, chapter 5, will conclude this research project and present implications for further study.

---

40. See Appendix X.

Chapter 5

Conclusions and Implications for Further Study

Introduction

DUE TO THE SPARSE amount of research and writing related to women and sexual shame, this doctoral dissertation surveyed Christian women to see how they have experienced sexual shame and how they have found freedom. Each survey participant wrote stories of pain, but many wrote stories of freedom.

In chapter 5, the researcher will explain the interpretation of the results, provide conclusions related to the hypotheses, and list implications for ministry—specifically, how the church can create safe biblical community through Sexual Discipleship to help free women from sexual shame.

Interpretation of Results and Conclusions

The research project showed that most women are experiencing sexual shame (61.93 percent "Agree" or "Strongly agree"), while only 31.56 percent "Agree" or "Strongly agree" that they are free from sexual shame. Shame reduction is necessary for women to heal from their sexual issues. Sadly, some women (13.12 percent) are even leaving their church or Christian communities because of it. Not only is being in Christian community important, but leaving it becomes problematic for women struggling with sexual shame. The research showed that going to church and being in a Christian community helps increase freedom from sexual shame (see figures 14 and 15). If women leave the church, they may not find freedom.

Sexual shame is also causing women to live secret lives and hide activities from friends and family (52.11 percent). Sexual shame is preventing women from being fully known and fully loved. Isolating from others and keeping their pain to themselves is problematic, because 43.21 percent of participants agreed that sharing their struggles with other believers helped to free them from sexual shame. If women leave their church or Christian community, they may not find empathetic friends or intimate connections to others, both of which, participants indicated, were sources that brought freedom from shame.

Possibly the most important issue that this survey brought out is that sexual shame leads to theological doubts and unbelief that conflicts with a woman's relationship with God. Sexual shame made 68.99 percent of women feel far from God. If God feels far away, women might not realize that they can turn to him, confess, and ask for forgiveness from their sexual sins (1 John 1:9). In fact, 34.40 percent of the women believe that their sins cannot be forgiven. These statistics show that women lack an understanding of God's omnipresence and fail to understand that God will never leave them nor forsake them (Deut 31:6). Even more worrisome, the survey showed that sexual shame caused 29.45 percent of women to doubt their salvation. These women felt so worthless that they believed it discredited them from entering the kingdom of God and that their sins were beyond the power of the cross. No longer does the issue of sexual shame destroy the present, but sexual shame may change a woman's view of eternity. Christian leaders can help women understand the theology that they are saved by grace, not by works, and that only through Christ can one become righteous (Eph 2:8–9; 2 Cor 5:21).

Because of sexual shame, women doubt God loves them (42.29 percent) and feel like God rejects them (35.96 percent). As

Conclusions and Implications for Further Study

a result, they avoid spending time with him by reading the Bible (41.83 percent) or spending time in prayer (46.06 percent). Even if women do cry out to God in prayer, 34.31 percent believe that God will not hear their prayers because of their sexual shame. Doubting that God will hear their prayers is problematic, because this research project shows that those who pray to God every day feel an average of 62.61 percent free from sexual shame. Additionally, the more a participant studied the Bible, the freer she felt from sexual shame (see figure 13). Spending time with God through prayer and Bible study will help grow a woman's relationship with God and provide freedom from sexual shame. Sadly, however, sexual shame is actually preventing women from turning to the sources that will help them find freedom, and more importantly, keeping them from having an intimate relationship with God.

Helping people find freedom may look different for women of different ages. When correlating the ages of the participants to how they experience freedom from sexual shame (see table 6), those older than forty-one had lower percentages in each category. The lower percentages do not mean that older women are less free, but rather that they find freedom in different ways from younger women. This research project did not try to prove this claim, but two possible reasons that the older women did not experience freedom in similar ways could be that they are less active in their pursuit of freedom or that they are more uncomfortable talking about their struggles.

To help normalize the topic of sexual shame, churches and ministries need to talk about sexual shame and sexual issues more than a one-time conversation or a once-a-year sermon on sex, because there are women in every church struggling with sexual shame. The most common themes of stories from the participants included stories of experiencing sexual shame within sexual abuse or assault and stories of sexual shame surrounding pornography and masturbation. Pastors can no longer remain silent on these issues, nor can they address only men in these conversations. From this research, evidence has shown that important conversations about sex are not happening, since participants said either their church was silent on the topic or they heard only negative messages. The way to change the Christian community and help more women find freedom from sexual shame is through Sexual Discipleship. How to do Sexual Discipleship practically in ministry will be explored later in the chapter.

From this research, one can see that the previous literature review aligns with this research project in that sexual shame causes women to isolate from others and God and creates a fear of being known. Since women find freedom from being known in community, Christian leaders must start with helping women get to the root of their shame and must help them find freedom from these doubts and fears to get them into community. Reducing sexual shame may reduce unwanted sexual behaviors.

Conclusions Related to the Hypotheses

Hypothesis 1

Hypothesis 1 states, "Christian women will identify understanding the love and grace of God as a key factor in finding freedom from sexual shame."

The data greatly supported Hypothesis 1 in both the quantitative survey and the stories from the qualitative survey. The quantitative survey revealed that the most chosen answer to what biblical source or spiritual action provides freedom from sexual shame is "Reminding myself of God's love" (see figure 11). A close second is "Understanding all my sins (including shameful sexual acts) are forgiven through Christ's death." Another highly selected answer on the survey was "Acknowledgement of God's forgiveness for my sexual past." When Q10 was correlated with the ages of the participants, the highest percentage remained "Reminding myself of God's love." No matter the age of a person, she can find freedom by knowing God's love.

Since so many women doubted God's love and doubted their salvation, it is important for Christian women to learn more about God's character, his love and grace, to find healing. For example,

Conclusions and Implications for Further Study

5.41 percent of the women in the quantitative survey had an abortion, which is 59 women out of the total of 1,090. As mentioned before, women who have had abortions experience a religious abortion stigma and doubt that God loves and forgives them. This research similarly demonstrated that 44 percent of women who aborted doubted God's love, and 27 percent doubted their salvation. When the same fifty-nine women were correlated with how they found freedom from sexual shame, 74.58 percent said, "Reminding myself of God's love," and 76.27 percent said, "Knowing I have salvation through faith in Christ." The survey also revealed that 88.14 percent said they found freedom by "Acknowledgement of God's forgiveness for my sexual past." Exploring the responses of the participants who had an abortion is just one example of how knowing God's character will help free women from sexual shame. Another example is shown from a correlation with those who experience sexual shame due to "Being abused." Megan, a twenty-three-year-old participant in the qualitative survey, wrote about how her sexual abuse changed her view of God: "I wonder how God could have allowed such [the abuse] to happen to me. This started me on a journey of self-loathing."[1] She believed she was "damaged goods," which kept her from finding healing from her sexual trauma and, ultimately, healing in Christ. Similarly, 318 participants in the quantitative survey said they felt sexual shame from being abused (29.17 percent). For those women to find freedom, 76 percent had to remind themselves of God's love.

Hypothesis 2

Hypothesis 2 states, "Christian women will identify being known in biblical community as a key factor in finding freedom from sexual shame."

As with the first hyphothesis, the data greatly supported Hypothesis 2. The more a participant attended church or was a part of a Christian community, the freer that participant felt from

---

1. See Appendix Y.

sexual shame (see figure 14). Women need community to hear and believe that they are loved, no matter what they have done or what has been done to them. They need to experience empathy and vulnerability through intimate relationships with others. The survey revealed that 42.66 percent of the participants found freedom through a sense of belonging in community. Additionally, the number-one theme from the responses in the open-ended question in the qualitative survey was being known in biblical community.

When looking at the non-biblical sources that provide freedom in the quantitative survey, the top three were as follows: "Empathetic friendships," "Sharing my struggles with other believers," and "Intimate connection to others." All three of these answers reflect participation in biblical community. Similarly, Brown's research found that women will experience more freedom from shame when they are given opportunities to share their stories and to be met with acceptance and belonging in community.[2]

Interestingly, those nineteen to twenty-two years old and twenty-three to thirty years old chose the top three responses ("Empathetic friendships," "Sharing my struggles with other believers," and "Intimate connection to others") more than any other age range. Thus, women nineteen to twenty-two years old and twenty-three to thirty years old have experienced the healing power of a biblical community more often than other generations. Possibly, older women did not see the same value in authentic community as the younger women, which are made up of millennials and Generation Z.

Similar to Brown's research on empathy cited in chapter 2,[3] some women need to find healing from the same source from which they experienced the pain. For example, 270 participants experienced sexual shame from condemnatory comments from family members. Fifty-three percent of these women experienced freedom from "A sense of belonging in community." Out of those same 270 women, 51.85 percent found healing from "Sharing my

2. Brown, *I Thought*, 47, 59.
3. Brown, "Shame Resilience Theory," 41.

Conclusions and Implications for Further Study

struggles with other believers" and "Intimate connections to others." Similarly, 394 participants said sexual shame caused them to "Avoid authentic friendships," but 47.46 percent found freedom from "Intimate connections to others." Sadly, sexual shame will often lead women away from the very sources needed to bring them freedom and healing.

Hypothesis 3

Hypothesis 3 states, "Christian women will identify learning a biblical teaching of sexuality as a key factor in finding freedom from sexual shame."

While the data showed some support of Hypothesis 3, there is room for Christian leaders to grow in the area of offering biblical teaching. For Hypothesis 3, biblical teaching was not as frequently mentioned as a source of healing compared to Hypotheses 1 and 2, possibly because Sexual Discipleship has not been commonly practiced by believers. The lack of Sexual Discipleship is seen in the survey data in that only 14.13 percent of women marked "My church's teaching about biblical sexuality" as a source that brought them freedom. However, the results show that 64.86 percent of participants selected "Understanding that God created humans as sexual beings"—which is the fourth-highest answer to what biblical source or spiritual actions brought freedom. The low percentage of women who found freedom from their church's teaching and the high percentage of women who found healing from understanding a theology of sex shows that the women are most likely learning about biblical sexuality on their own, apart from the church or sermons. This makes sense, because many women listed Christian books and blogs in the "Other" categories for Q9 and Q10. Because of the lack of conversations occurring in churches, ministries such as Authentic Intimacy were created to train leaders and partner with churches to help them begin Sexual Discipleship in their congregations.

When "Understanding that God created humans as sexual beings" as a source of freedom (see table 6) was correlated with age, younger women averaged higher percentages than older women. The younger generations all averaged higher than 66 percent, while those forty-one and older averaged in the 50 percent range. Possibly, the younger generations are having conversations and pursuing biblical truth about sexuality more than the older generations.

The researcher also correlated the ages with those who selected "My church's teaching about biblical sexuality" as a source of freedom. For participants age sixty-six and older, 5.88 percent selected "My church's teaching about biblical sexuality," and 31.25 percent of those fourteen to eighteen years old selected "My church's teaching about biblical sexuality." While 30 percent is still a small amount, it is more than five times greater than that of the oldest generation of participants.

This research project has shown that the three hypotheses work best as a part of Sexual Discipleship, the key to stopping sexual shame from developing and bringing healing for those with sexual shame. Practical ways to begin Sexual Discipleship will be addressed in the implications section.

Sources of Additional Freedom Not Included on the Survey

Both surveys revealed an unexpected result based on the answers to the open-ended and "Other" questions. The participants listed additional sources of freedom which were not included on the survey. The number-one most mentioned source was a loving and supportive spouse. Words used by participants to describe the characteristics of a supportive husband included "patient," "loving," "listener," "understanding," and "encouraging."

Many women talked about the action of working together on their sexual shame with their husbands. Some ways that the women actively pursued freedom together with their husbands included the following: "Praying together," "Discussing my feelings openly with my Christian husband," and "Growing in spiritual intimacy and physical intimacy with my husband." In addition to working

Conclusions and Implications for Further Study

together, women also mentioned the healing power of confessing or sharing their story with their husbands and being met with love and forgiveness. One woman wrote, "Having a husband who forgave me and never judged me," and another said, "Knowing that my husband forgives me for my past and still loves me." It may be difficult for women to tell their painful story to their husbands, especially if they experienced shame from sharing in the past. One participant told her abuse story to her husband before they married, and she said, "His grace-filled response was amazing."

The spouse's loving comments can also help a woman find freedom from body shame (42.29 percent of participants felt sexual shame because of their bodies, and 51.10 percent said they felt shame about their body image). The spouse's support is important, because the better one felt about herself, her body, and her worth, the freer she felt from sexual shame.

Other research corroborates the finding that having a supportive spouse is a source of healing from sexual shame. Researcher and author Gregoire wrote about a woman who had body-shame and body-image issues who said that her husband saved their marriage by combatting every negative lie in her head and replacing them with positive truths about sex, her body, and his love for her. The woman said that for fifteen years, her husband would "tell me every day, 'I find you beautiful, I find you attractive, you are not lacking in anything, and what your body looks like is what I want and need.'"[4] These comments from her husband helped her to break free from body and sexual shame and to experience sexual intimacy with her husband the way God intended.

Because of the gender stereotypes that many women have mentioned hearing from their churches, it makes sense that a wife would need the loving support of a husband to break free from the sexual shame such lies have caused.

The following implications reflect the opinions of the survey participants.

---

4. Gregoire et al., *Great Sex Rescue*, 208.

Implications for Ministry

This research project revealed how women experience sexual shame and how they find freedom. There is a need for churches to begin Sexual Discipleship in order to help women find freedom. Women struggle with sexual issues, so Christian leaders need to talk about these topics in their communities—in sermons or small-group-curriculum discussion questions. The church cannot remain silent. Instead of a one-time conversation, leaders can think of Sexual Discipleship as a lifelong approach. Through Sexual Discipleship, Christians can discover what they believe about sexuality through the Bible, how such truths relate to life and living, and how to help the next generation follow God with their sexuality.[5]

How Can the Church Begin Sexual Discipleship?

Create a Safe Place in Church to Talk about Sexuality

Survey participants stated they had no safe place to ask questions about sex or to talk about sexuality. Having a safe place is a part of biblical community. What is not safe includes victim blaming (versus a mindset of believing women when they come forward), rape myths, and labeling sexual issues as "men's issues." Churches need to create a safe place for couples to come forward for help with affairs and sexual addictions. One way to offer a safe place is to have women staff members and/or trained lay leaders so that women are able to speak with other women.

Instead of silencing or shaming women, churches can talk about pain in sex and normalize these conversations. Since 52.11 percent of participants live secret lives because of their sexual shame, these women might never have experienced a safe place to talk about their issues. If the church started conversations about the topics mentioned in this project, these women could come forward instead of keeping secrets. Safe places offer empathetic

---

5. Slattery, *Rethinking Sexuality*, 31.

Conclusions and Implications for Further Study

friendships and places where others can begin talking about their struggles and sharing their stories with other believers. Women can also ask questions about sexuality and learn how to find answers. Safe places create a place of belonging.

Start with the Issue of Sexual Shame

Instead of beginning with behavior modification, Christian leaders can first help women heal from sexual shame. Since this study showed that sexual shame leads to many sexual sins, Christian leaders should start with heart change through discipleship.

Learn and Teach Biblical Sexuality

The survey revealed that 27.27 percent of participants stated they never heard their pastors or families talk about sexuality or left the question blank. Churches can use the Sexual Discipleship method instead of the silence or education approach. Churches need to first understand what the Bible says about sexuality and then teach people in their communities the truths. Biblical sexuality does not include sexist comments or stereotypes. God created sex and sexual desire for both men and women as a part of God's good design. By teaching biblical sexuality and education, Christians can help marriages close the orgasm gap.[6] Many women in the surveys wrote that they experienced sexual shame from lack of orgasms in sexual intimacy.

Teaching biblical sexuality means communicating that God created both men and women as image bearers. Unfortunately, 31.93 percent of women said "My church's view on women" made/makes them experience sexual shame. Women are not second-class citizens to men, but are created with equal worth and dignity

---

6. Research shows that only 48.7 percent of women always or almost always reach orgasm during sexual encounters with their husband (Gregoire et al., *Great Sex Rescue*, 41). While for men, research has found that over 90 percent of men always or almost always orgasm (Wade et al., "Incidental Orgasm," 117–38).

as men. Explain that a woman's body, no matter what she is wearing, does not make her a stumbling block that will "destroy men's pursuit of holiness or serve as invitation for assault."[7] Church leaders can begin changing the messaging and language around women and men.

Understand that Sexual Issues are Spiritual Issues[8]

This research showed that women found freedom from their sexual issue by better understanding the gospel. Pastors can learn to integrate spirituality and sexuality. Women's sexual issues could have underlying wrong theology. To find freedom, the women needed to know God loved them and forgave them despite their sexual sin and shame. These biblical truths were chosen more than any other biblical source or spiritual action to free women from sexual shame. Thus, Christian leaders need to spend time talking about God's love through Christ's death, and the fact that forgiveness and salvation come through Jesus in regard to sexual issues. Nothing one has done, including shameful sexual acts, is too far gone to be forgiven by Jesus Christ. Salvation is through Christ, not by ones' own works.

Talk about Biblical Sexuality for Singles and Married People

Many participants said they heard sexuality discussed only for married couples, which brought more shame for singles. Christian leaders should value singleness equally to how much they value marriage. Marriage is not the goal of a believer. The goal is for people to become more like Christ. Also, leaders can help those dating and engaged to navigate relationships and conversations to prevent more sexual shame from entering into the marriage.

---

7. Bluhm, *Prey Tell*, 140.
8. Slattery, *Rethinking Sexuality*, 15.

Conclusions and Implications for Further Study

This study showed how many participants did not enjoy sexual intimacy with their husbands, and a few wrote that their sexual shame was from sexual activities before marriage. Yet, the research also showed the value of a supportive spouse in the freedom journey. Christian leaders can help restore marriages by educating the couples on how to work together to remove sexual shame.

Include Positive Messages about Biblical Sexuality

The survey showed that 59.09 percent of participants heard only negative things about sexuality from their ministers and pastors. The church needs to preach a message that is more than "Just don't do it" or "You're going to hell if you have sex." Instead, leaders can preach about the beauty of God's design for sexuality, especially since "Understanding that God created humans as sexual beings" was ranked fourth highest on the list of biblical sources or spiritual actions that provided freedom for the women. God created his people as sexual beings, and their sexual desires are good.

Teach Parents How to Talk about Sex with their Children

More than 70 percent (70.45 percent) of participants said that sex was never talked about in the home. Church leaders need to encourage parents to sexually disciple their children and talk about sexuality at home, more than a one-time conversation. Parents should learn the accurate terms for body parts to include in conversations about sexuality.

Help Women Improve Body Image and View of Self

Women may improve their view of self when church leaders help them to see the value in their bodies and sexuality. More than 50 percent (51.1 percent) of women said "My poor body image" made/makes them experience sexual shame, and 42.29 percent said a source of sexual shame was "My body." Christian leaders need to help women improve their view of self and their body by valuing the woman's body as more than something to be used.⁹

Implications for Future Research

Additional research questions could be studied to expand ministry and knowledge about sexual shame. These include:

- Does sexual shame cause sexual sin and addiction or do sexual sin and addiction cause sexual shame?
- Is there a direct link between sexual shame and pornography use?
- How does sexual shame affect a woman's sexual intimacy in marriage?
- How can husbands partner with their wives in their journey to freedom from sexual shame?
- How can Sexual Discipleship be tested in churches as a before-and-after research study?
- How can a woman improve her body image and view of self in order to grow in freedom from sexual shame?
- How can churches create safe biblical communities where empathetic friendships can grow and people can talk openly about their struggles in order to free people from sexual shame?

---

9. In her book *Prey Tell*, Tiffany Bluhm talks about how to free women from body shame. She states, "We must overhaul how we think about women's bodies as something to be used or abused and put a full stop to victim blaming. The presumption that women are to be damsels in distress (purity-culture) or to be dominated (rape culture) paints women as prey, not as equals with agency to determine what happens to their bodies or lives. Interestingly, purity-culture and rape culture have always had one notion in common: that a woman's body is not her own but belongs to a man" (Bluhm, *Prey Tell*, 93).

Conclusions and Implications for Further Study

Conclusion

Based on the research results, a high percentage of women have experienced sexual shame. Three key influences in helping them find freedom are the following: understanding the love and grace of God, being known in biblical community, and learning a biblical teaching of sexuality.

Appendix A
Qualitative Survey Questions

1. Do I have your permission to use this survey in my research project and future books? Your name would be changed so that you would remain anonymous. Yes/No
2. In what year were you born? (Enter four-digit birth year; for example, 1976.)
3. Are you a follower of Jesus Christ? Yes/No
4. Have you ever experienced sexual shame? Please share your story (open-ended).
5. What helped you find freedom from sexual shame (open-ended)?
6. What are specific things you've heard ministers say about sexuality that brought more shame than good (open-ended)?
7. Please check off which of the following that you have struggled with.
    - Promiscuity
    - Lust
    - Homosexuality
    - Masturbation
    - Pornography

8. Share how your family talked about sex in the home. Were they comfortable with it? Were you shamed for sexual thoughts, questions, or behaviors in the home (open-ended)?
9. Is there anything else you want to share about your story (open-ended)?

Appendix B
Quantitative Survey Questions

Q1: Are you a female who gives me permission to use this survey in my research project and future writing?

- Yes
- No

Q2: What is your age?

- 13 or younger
- 14–18
- 19–22
- 23–30
- 31–40
- 41–50
- 51–65
- 65 or older

Sexual Shame in Women and How to Experience Freeedom

Q3: Please indicate how often you do the following:

	Never	A few times per year	Once or twice per month	Once or twice per week	Every day
I attend church					
I study the Bible (either alone, with a mentor, or in a small group)					
I pray to God					
I am in a Christian community where biblical topics are discussed					

Q4: Use the scale below to grade how accurately the statements reflect your life:

	Strongly disagree	Disagree	Indifferent	Somewhat agree	Agree	Strongly agree
I feel good about who I am						
I feel worthwhile and valuable						
I am content in my relationship status						
I love myself						
I experience sexual shame						
I am free from sexual shame						

Q5: How free do you feel from sexual shame?

Open-ended question to enter a number from zero to one hundred.

Appendix B

Q6: In the past, sexual shame has caused me to do the following (please check all that apply):

- Leave my church or Christian community
- Feel far from God
- Turn to pornography
- Masturbate
- Avoid authentic friendships
- Doubt my salvation
- Doubt God's love for me
- Feel that my sins cannot be forgiven by God
- Avoid reading Scripture
- Avoid prayer
- Feel that God rejects me
- Fear God will not hear my prayers
- Live a secret life; hide my activities from friends and family
- Other (please specify)

Q7: What sexual acts made/make me experience sexual shame (please check all that apply)?

- Looking at pornography
- Same-sex attraction
- Masturbation
- Sexual intercourse outside of marriage
- Nonintercourse-related sexual contact (e.g., fondling, oral sex)
- Taking advantage of others
- Being abused
- Regular one-night stands or hookups
- Sexual fantasies or lust that interfere with my life
- Other (please specify)

Q8: What other factors made/make me experience sexual shame (please check all that apply)?

- My pastor's sermons
- Condemnatory comments from family
- Condemnatory comments from friends
- Treatment for a sexually transmitted disease
- I have an incurable sexually transmitted disease
- I had an abortion
- My church's view of women
- My body
- My poor body image
- Other (please specify)

Q9: What non-biblical sources free me from my sexual shame (please check all that apply)?

- Secular counseling
- Christian counseling
- Online support groups or recovery groups
- Face-to-face support or recovery groups
- Empathetic friendships
- Self-help books
- Mindfulness practice
- Ignoring the shame
- Intimate connections to others
- Forgetting my past
- Nothing
- Sharing my struggles with other believers
- Other (please specify)

Appendix B

Q10: What biblical sources or spiritual actions free me from my sexual shame (please check all that apply)?

- ◻ Acknowledgement of God's forgiveness for my sexual past
- ◻ Knowing that I have salvation through faith in Christ
- ◻ Understanding that God created humans as sexual beings
- ◻ Understanding all my sins (including shameful sexual acts) are forgiven through Christ's death
- ◻ Obeying God's guidelines from the Bible
- ◻ Reminding myself of God's love
- ◻ My church's teaching about biblical sexuality
- ◻ Regular Bible study
- ◻ Prayer
- ◻ A sense of belonging in community
- ◻ Other (please specify)

Appendix C
Francesca (Participant #21)

Q1. Do I have your permission to use this survey in my research project and future books? Your name would be changed so that you would remain anonymous.

- Yes

Q2. In what year were you born? (Enter four-digit birth year; for example, 1976.)

- 1993

Q3. Are you a follower of Jesus Christ?

- Yes

Q4. Have you ever experienced sexual shame? Please share your story.

- Yes. I have struggled with porn addiction, masturbation, lust, and promiscuity.

Q5. What helped you find freedom from sexual shame?

- Being able to talk to other women about things I am usually ashamed to talk about.

Q6. What are specific things you've heard ministers say about sexuality that brought more shame than good?

Appendix C

- Having sex before marriage ruins your marriage. Silence about sex and women's desire for sex.

Q7. Please check off which of the following that you have struggled with.

- Pornography
- Masturbation
- Lust
- Promiscuity

Q8. Share how your family talked about sex in the home. Were they comfortable with it? Were you shamed for sexual thoughts, questions, or behaviors in the home?

- My family did not talk about sex. They only referred to it in biblical references. I did not share with them my sexual thoughts and behaviors. There was no safe space to ask questions about sex.

Q9. Is there anything else you want to share about your story?

- Respondent skipped this question.

Appendix D
Ashley (Participant #9)

Q1. Do I have your permission to use this survey in my research project and future books? Your name would be changed so that you would remain anonymous.

- Yes

Q2. In what year were you born? (Enter four-digit birth year; for example, 1976.)

- 1990

Q3. Are you a follower of Jesus Christ?

- Yes

Q4. Have you ever experienced sexual shame? Please share your story.

- I have experienced shame for wanting to be admired/desired sensually and sexually when I was in college. In marriage, I experience great shame for not enjoying or desiring sex. I have found freedom from the shame I experienced in my college years by placing my hope for emotional fulfillment and satisfaction in Christ alone. I currently continue to experience immense shame for not enjoying or desiring sex with my husband, whom I love.

Appendix D

Q5. What helped you find freedom from sexual shame?

- Christ alone.

Q6. What are specific things you've heard ministers say about sexuality that brought more shame than good?

- I understood the complete lack of talking/educating young Christians in sex/sexuality as what made sex appear shameful.

Q7. Please check off which of the following that you have struggled with.

- Lust

Q8. Share how your family talked about sex in the home. Were they comfortable with it? Were you shamed for sexual thoughts, questions, or behaviors in the home?

- We never talked about sex and it was regarded as bad behavior. My dad was chastised by my mom for calling her sexy. I was rebuked for using the word vagina.

Q9. Is there anything else you want to share about your story?

- No

Appendix E

Brooklyn (Participant #16)

Q1. Do I have your permission to use this survey in my research project and future books? Your name would be changed so that you would remain anonymous.

- Yes

Q2. In what year were you born? (Enter four-digit birth year; for example, 1976.)

- 1993

Q3. Are you a follower of Jesus Christ?

- Yes

Q4. Have you ever experienced sexual shame? Please share your story.

- Yes. I was molested by a cousin at a young age. I never understood what he was doing to me but years later as a young adult I realized how he had taken advantage of me. I found myself numb to the circumstances; the numbness over time turned into a deep sadness mixed with a lot of confusion (in regards to people and their sexual choices). Also, I was very "sexual" on my own growing up. I secretly masturbated and sometimes watched sensual scenes from movies to make me feel "good." I always felt ashamed and dirty after doing

Appendix E

these things and even have tried to shower the dirty shameful feelings I would get after it all. Despite my guilt, I would find myself engaging in the same sins after a few days. I also struggled with same sex attraction and would fantasize about things I knew were evil in the sight of God. And yet again, despite the shame and frustrations I would experience, I would find myself dabbling in the same perversions time after time. I never told anyone these things—especially not at church. I was crippled by my desire for other females and felt left out in conversations with my other girlfriends (believers and nonbelievers alike) who liked guys. I tried to surrender it all to God a million times and secretly desired to be attracted to males, but rarely found the courage to speak up and be honest about my struggles.

Q5. What helped you find freedom from sexual shame?

- Verbally speaking about my shame was the first step in helping me find freedom. It was embarrassing but speaking the words to another human being made my shame feel more real which then brings about other possibilities beyond the shame and hurt. Every time I shared to someone about my stories & struggles, I felt less alone and a little more accepted as a human. This eventually helped me speak to God more honestly about my shame and also pushed me to actually obey the Scriptures and intently battle with the thoughts in my mind.

Q6. What are specific things you've heard ministers say about sexuality that brought more shame than good?

- Scriptures about women being gentle. That confused me; I wasn't very "gentle"—I was tomboyish and slightly loud and clumsy. I knew ministers meant "gentle" in a way that reflected a woman's heart. But I was still confused because I wasn't very woman-like according to the social norm—add that with my same sex struggles and I was extra lost.

Q7. Please check off which of the following that you have struggled with.

- Pornography
- Masturbation
- Homosexuality
- Lust

Q8. Share how your family talked about sex in the home. Were they comfortable with it? Were you shamed for sexual thoughts, questions, or behaviors in the home?

- Never talked about any of it.

Q9. Is there anything else you want to share about your story?

- Joy, you're awesome.

Appendix F
Tanisha (Participant #34)

Q1. Do I have your permission to use this survey in my research project and future books? Your name would be changed so that you would remain anonymous.

- Yes

Q2. In what year were you born? (Enter four-digit birth year; for example, 1976.)

- 1987

Q3. Are you a follower of Jesus Christ?

- Yes

Q4. Have you ever experienced sexual shame? Please share your story.

- Being a virgin in my mid 30s has been very difficult even with dating men who are in the church and relationships with family who know your sexual history (or lack thereof). Throughout the years, in situations where the relationship was getting more serious, that is when I would share my desire to wait until marriage. And I purposely decided to date professed Christian men thinking it may [be] easier. It has definitely not! It has usually resulted in the ending of relationships not moving to the exclusive phrase. Even Christian men felt uncomfortable dating a woman who is "inexperienced" or deemed to be "asexual." And this has been my experience with men in the church even ministers! Not only that I have had family send me condoms because they considered my decision to wait to be "unrealistic." The church has not been much support because usually the "waiting until marriage" talks stops and support to navigate this part of your life stops at maybe college ministry. By then it's usually assumed that you will be married by the time you are in your 30s. No one discusses how you will be perceived by your family thinking you some sexually repressed weirdo. Or that your dating prospects will be slim to none, and you constantly are subjected to shame and downright embarrassing conversations with men who just don't quite get you have been "waiting for so long." Wondering if you even made the right decision at all or should just wait to have sex in a committed relationship. My struggle has not been giving in to temptation but to be rid of the shame and stigma attached to waiting.

Q5. What helped you find freedom from sexual shame?

- Having some of my closest friends who are waiting where we hold each other accountable has helped. I have had to pray, get clear on why I am continuing to wait, and be intentional about what I want. I have also had to reprioritize myself and love myself and not allow the opinions or perception of men and family stop me from making decisions that are God honoring choices and well being.

Q6. What are specific things you've heard ministers say about sexuality that brought more shame than good?

- I know from experience that I was shamed into waiting. Hearing in youth group that you're going to hell if you have sex. Having sexual needs and desires are all lumped into the "lust category" that you need "deliverance."

Appendix F

Q7. Please check off which of the following that you have struggled with.

- Respondent skipped this question.

Q8. Share how your family talked about sex in the home. Were they comfortable with it? Were you shamed for sexual thoughts, questions, or behaviors in the home?

- My Dad NEVER talked to me about it. My mom allowed me to ask any questions that I had when I was 12 but that was about it.

Q9. Is there anything else you want to share about your story?

- No that's it.

Appendix G
Grace (Participant #28)

Q1. Do I have your permission to use this survey in my research project and future books? Your name would be changed so that you would remain anonymous.

- Yes

Q2. In what year were you born? (Enter four-digit birth year; for example, 1976.)

- 1992

Q3. Are you a follower of Jesus Christ?

- Yes

Q4. Have you ever experienced sexual shame? Please share your story.

- I grew up being emotionally and verbally bullied by boys, so when I got older I guess I sought their attention and approval. I sent my first nude photos when I was 14 years old. I was hooked on the attention and praise I got from any boys who lusted after me, even though I knew deep down that it wasn't real love. I wanted to feel desirable. Out of curiosity, I started looking at porn and I developed a porn addiction when I was 18 years old. Those same boys I sent nudes to also got me into sexting and playing out fantasies in my mind.

Appendix G

My first boyfriend was sexually active with me even though we were both Christians, and he knew I watched porn but he didn't seem worried about it. Even with a boyfriend, I was still sexting with other guys in secret. My boyfriend's attention wasn't enough for me. Later he found out what I was doing and dumped me. We were together for 3 years, so losing him felt like a huge loss. It hurt. After moving on from our break-up, I still had a porn addiction. About 4 years later, I was rejected by a friend of mine, someone I liked and confessed feelings for. The pain from that rejection drove me to seek comfort from more than just porn. The porn wasn't enough anymore. It was then that I developed a sex addiction as well. I was hooking up with strangers for about a year and a half. I was still watching porn, but finding a new sex partner was the most thrilling thing for me at the time. After having sex, I would feel a huge wave of depression and shame. Every time. I especially felt ashamed after I found out that I got chlamydia. I had no idea who I got it from or how long I had it, but thankfully I had health insurance, so I was able to get treated. That was one of the things that made me realize how low I had gotten.

Q5. What helped you find freedom from sexual shame?

- I was tired of feeling so much guilt and shame. I was living a double life. I was still going to church and serving in our high school ministry, teaching teenage girls about God. I felt unworthy to be there. I wanted to be a better example. I knew that if it's true that God loves me, He wouldn't want me to live the way I had been living. I felt convicted by the Holy Spirit to seek help. I knew deep down that I couldn't really heal by myself, even though I was afraid of others judging me and rejecting me for the things I had done. I finally confessed out loud for the first time that I had a porn and sex addiction to one of the pastors at my church. I was sobbing as I did it, but I found a sort of freedom by finally exposing my addiction. My pastor was compassionate and gracious. I learned that he too suffered from a porn addiction when he was younger. He encouraged me to talk to one of the women at church who I served alongside with, so I did. She became my accountability partner, and we meet once a week from then on. Not only did I find someone who I could confide in, an accountability partner who is older and wiser than me, but I also made a friend in her. I was surprised by how much she related to me, how she knows exactly what it is to seek attention from guys and wanting to feel wanted. Having someone to talk to and be with me on my journey of recovery is amazing. After doing some online research, I was also able to find a support group at one of my local churches for women who suffer from love and sex addiction. I recently just started going to my support group, and I know it's the right place for me. I'm still healing, and my progress isn't perfect, but it is progress. I have never regretted my decision to confess about my addiction. I'm so glad I did. Ever since, God has come through and He has shown me that He is with me through this whole thing.

Q6. What are specific things you've heard ministers say about sexuality that brought more shame than good?

- The way they emphasize that struggle with lust and porn addiction is more of a "man's thing." It made me feel like a freak. The way they say men need to "resist" their temptations while women need to be "modest" and "pure" as if we have no temptations to stay away from, too.

Q7. Please check off which of the following that you have struggled with.

- Pornography
- Masturbation
- Lust
- Promiscuity

Appendix G

Q8. Share how your family talked about sex in the home. Were they comfortable with it? Were you shamed for sexual thoughts, questions, or behaviors in the home?

- My mom always warned us that we better not get pregnant or get anyone else pregnant. That was the extent of the sex talk in our home. Just don't get pregnant. While I was being promiscuous, I was living at home, and I knew my parents could tell what I was doing. They didn't talk about it with me but they gave disapproving looks and had condescending tones in their voice. I felt very ashamed, especially because they know I'm a Christian so I felt judged for my behavior.

Q9. Is there anything else you want to share about your story?

- Respondent skipped this question.

Appendix H
Jessica (Participant #6)

Q1. Do I have your permission to use this survey in my research project and future books? Your name would be changed so that you would remain anonymous.

- Yes

Q2. In what year were you born? (Enter four-digit birth year; for example, 1976.)

- 1995

Q3. Are you a follower of Jesus Christ?

- Yes

Q4. Have you ever experienced sexual shame? Please share your story.

- Yes, I was exposed to pornography as a first grader by a childhood friend and had no idea the lasting effects it would have on me as I got older. While I didn't understand what it was or why it was bad, I innately felt that it was wrong and that alone filled me with plenty of shame. As I got older I curiously surfed the tv channels late at night and would find similar content to what I saw that very first night. While finishing up in high school it evolved from watching porn to masturbating and I always convinced myself it was harmless because it affected nobody but me. Little did I know it began to affect my thought life in some very intense ways which evolved into lust in my heart and mind. The shame followed me through life with its foot on my throat until the first time I heard someone else share that they too struggled with it and that defeated the biggest lie that I knew at the time which was that I was in this alone.

Q5. What helped you find freedom from sexual shame?

- Hearing other women talk openly about it. Learning about the neurological patterns for addiction and how to break it. Diving into the word of God to learn what He says about sex and sexuality. Having churches affirm issues just like this as equal in sin nature to the rest. Focusing on God's grace and his new mercies for me every day, even on the days I mess up. Learning to fight and setting up a relapse plan.

Q6. What are specific things you've heard ministers say about sexuality that brought more shame than good?

- Hearing that only men struggled with pornography/masturbation/lust communicated to me as a woman that I was some form of alien and needed to remain silent to keep myself safe.

Q7. Please check off which of the following that you have struggled with.

- Pornography
- Masturbation
- Lust

Q8. Share how your family talked about sex in the home. Were they comfortable with it? Were you shamed for sexual thoughts, questions, or behaviors in the home?

- They didn't talk about sex so when I began having questions I did not feel comfortable asking anyone in my home. Culturally, my parents were comfortable with it and it was a normal thing that would take place eventually, but they didn't prioritize having open conversations about it and my grandmother especially viewed it as more taboo. All of which added to the self-placed shame I already had from my thoughts and actions.

Q9. Is there anything else you want to share about your story?

- The best advice I ever got was that my fear is not as great as someone else's freedom so I should use my voice and share my story any chance I get.

Appendix I
Wendy (Participant #26)

Q1. Do I have your permission to use this survey in my research project and future books? Your name would be changed so that you would remain anonymous.

- Yes

Q2. In what year were you born? (Enter four-digit birth year; for example, 1976.)

- 1988

Q3. Are you a follower of Jesus Christ?

- Yes

Q4. Have you ever experienced sexual shame? Please share your story.

- As a child I felt this underlying shame because of my sexuality. I would wear 3 sports bras so that my chest was flat, I wore boys' clothes so that no one would think I was too feminine, and I refused to even show my collar bone when wearing dresses because I saw my body as a stumbling block for men. I saw women as weak, having no power. Growing up I hated the fact that I was one, I was a part of the weaker sex. I was hurt that God made me into something so powerless. I don't know who to blame or point fingers at, I don't really think that has helped me in my healing. The last few years I've learned to walk through my story, it's a hard one, but a blessed one. I've learned to take responsibility for my choices and also not take on guilt that isn't mine. I am a new person now because in the last few years I've found my identity, and a huge part of my identity is being a woman. God made me into someone powerful, I'm proud of that. If I were talking to younger me, I would tell her to not accept or buy into what she saw. Have the courage to see herself as someone of value not based on anything in this world but on who God said she was. As a woman she was loved by God. No one else's opinion really matters but His.

Q5. What helped you find freedom from sexual shame?

- Going to counseling to work on identity issues and friendships that encouraged me to challenge my thoughts.

Q6. What are specific things you've heard ministers say about sexuality that brought more shame than good?

- "Men are all this way . . ." "Women are all this way . . ." "The female body is a stumbling block for all men and should be covered." "Men can't control themselves."

Q7. Please check off which of the following that you have struggled with.

- Lust

Q8. Share how your family talked about sex in the home. Were they comfortable with it? Were you shamed for sexual thoughts, questions, or behaviors in the home?

- Sex was seen as something to be reserved for marriage; we did talk about it. Personally, I hated talking about it with my parents because my mom had no boundaries. She was not safe. My brothers struggled with porn from very young ages and as a result of that amongst other things they were scape goats in the family.

Appendix I

Q9. Is there anything else you want to share about your story?

- Something I learned in my undergrad, while I had not struggled with sexual issues in the same way as many of my peers, one thing that was difficult to walk through was being the "inexperienced" one. Since then, I feel confident in my story, but back in college it wasn't just that I had chosen not to do certain behaviors, but back then I didn't feel that I was even loveable. It was hard to constantly be reminded how much I "didn't know about the world." The people saying those things were young and didn't know, but it still hurt. Something I've learned through my story is that not doing certain things doesn't necessarily mean you're in any way better, it could mean your issues are just different.

Appendix J
Holly (Participant #37)

Q1. Do I have your permission to use this survey in my research project and future books? Your name would be changed so that you would remain anonymous.

- Yes

Q2. In what year were you born? (Enter four-digit birth year; for example, 1976.)

- 1952

Q3. Are you a follower of Jesus Christ?

- Yes

Q4. Have you ever experienced sexual shame? Please share your story.

- I was molested as a young teen by a family member. Later, as a married women I had a lesbian relationship with a woman who had had relationships with teenage girls.

Q5. What helped you find freedom from sexual shame?

- I am just finding the freedom that Christ offers from [a] Christian therapist. She has directed me to the grace that is available in knowing God.

Appendix J

Q6. What are specific things you've heard ministers say about sexuality that brought more shame than good?

- Not sure I heard about it.

Q7. Please check off which of the following that you have struggled with.

- Pornography
- Masturbation
- Homosexuality

Q8. Share how your family talked about sex in the home. Were they comfortable with it? Were you shamed for sexual thoughts, questions, or behaviors in the home?

- Raised in non-Christian home. No real judgement except snickers about lesbian and gay relationship.

Q9. Is there anything else you want to share about your story?

- I feel my own lesbian relationship happened because she groomed me by listening to my feelings of shame and protected herself from my reporting her to authorities about her relationship with school girls as her coaching position.

Appendix K

Anna (Participant #22)

Q1. Do I have your permission to use this survey in my research project and future books? Your name would be changed so that you would remain anonymous.

- Yes

Q2. In what year were you born? (Enter four-digit birth year; for example, 1976.)

- 1979

Q3. Are you a follower of Jesus Christ?

- Yes

Q4. Have you ever experienced sexual shame? Please share your story.

- Yes and lots of it . . . including being sexually abused as a child as well as entering sinful and ungodly relationships in the past.

Q5. What helped you find freedom from sexual shame?

- Knowing that God forgives me and loves me.

Q6. What are specific things you've heard ministers say about sexuality that brought more shame than good?

Appendix K

- Honestly, I can't say I've really heard too much from Ministers in my life but I have heard about the importance of sexual purity.

Q7. Please check off which of the following that you have struggled with.

- Pornography
- Masturbation
- Lust

Q8. Share how your family talked about sex in the home. Were they comfortable with it? Were you shamed for sexual thoughts, questions, or behaviors in the home?

- I grew up in a non Christian [home] . . . I think that's it all really.

Q9. Is there anything else you want to share about your story?

- No

Appendix L
Andrea (Participant #20)

Q1. Do I have your permission to use this survey in my research project and future books? Your name would be changed so that you would remain anonymous.

- Yes

Q2. In what year were you born? (Enter four-digit birth year; for example, 1976.)

- 1984

Q3. Are you a follower of Jesus Christ?

- Yes

Q4. Have you ever experienced sexual shame? Please share your story.

- Yes—I slept with, and became pregnant by, a man who lived with his longterm girlfriend. That pregnancy was aborted and I went on to sleep with several other men after him. All of these decisions were against what I'd always believed in and to this day, I haven't revealed a lot of this information to people who know me. After I stopped dating/having sex, watching pornography and masturbating became a regular occurrence. I am now doing my best to live a pure life that doesn't include any of the above mentioned activities.

Appendix L

Q5. What helped you find freedom from sexual shame?

- God's forgiveness. The Freedom from Porn devotion on the Holy Bible app that led me to Joy Pedrow Ministries. Sharing with Christian friends who assured me of God's love and forgiveness. Ultimately, forgiving myself.

Q6. What are specific things you've heard ministers say about sexuality that brought more shame than good?

- How big of a sin sex outside of marriage is, how abortion is murder and the killing of God's children, how ashamed people should be when they're living outside of God's will for their lives, how people who live outside of God's will will burn in hell and won't be so happy about their sexual escapades then . . .

Q7. Please check off which of the following that you have struggled with.

- Pornography
- Masturbation
- Lust
- Promiscuity

Q8. Share how your family talked about sex in the home. Were they comfortable with it? Were you shamed for sexual thoughts, questions, or behaviors in the home?

- There was very little discussion of sex in my home growing up and when there was, it was just about how God intended it for marriage. We weren't allowed to joke about sexual things, or even come close, and open conversation was not something that occurred. I didn't share any of my situation with my parents until I was outed by another person who shared it with them.

Q9. Is there anything else you want to share about your story?

- A big part of what I was missing from my childhood was feeling truly loved and appreciated by my Dad and being taught how loving and forgiving God is. Not feeling loved by a man was a factor in my willingness to be with a man I shouldn't have been with. Not thinking God was so loving and forgiving led me to walk away from Him for years in an effort to ignore the judgement I thought was awaiting me.

Appendix M
Bailey (Participant #29)

Q1. Do I have your permission to use this survey in my research project and future books? Your name would be changed so that you would remain anonymous.

- Yes

Q2. In what year were you born? (Enter four-digit birth year; for example, 1976.)

- 1986

Q3. Are you a follower of Jesus Christ?

- Yes

Q4. Have you ever experienced sexual shame? Please share your story.

- Yes, I was molested when I was 9 by my mom's friend's nephews and did this for 4 years.

Q5. What helped you find freedom from sexual shame?

- With Christ['s] help, He showed me how He sees me and that He washed the shame away.

Q6. What are specific things you've heard ministers say about sexuality that brought more shame than good?

- Unwed pregnant mothers

Q7. Please check off which of the following that you have struggled with.

- Pornography
- Masturbation
- Homosexuality
- Lust
- Promiscuity

Q8. Share how your family talked about sex in the home. Were they comfortable with it? Were you shamed for sexual thoughts, questions, or behaviors in the home?

- No, my parents were not comfortable and kind of they were not sure how to answer the questions and allowed school to teach us.

Q9. Is there anything else you want to share about your story?

- No

Appendix N
Adaobi (Participant #14)

Q1. Do I have your permission to use this survey in my research project and future books? Your name would be changed so that you would remain anonymous.

- Yes

Q2. In what year were you born? (Enter four-digit birth year; for example, 1976.)

- 2000

Q3. Are you a follower of Jesus Christ?

- Yes

Q4. Have you ever experienced sexual shame? Please share your story.

- Growing up, I wanted to experience how it felt like to be loved. To have someone to hold you. I started early, looking for someone or something to fill the emptiness in my heart. I had a boyfriend in the last year of high school. We clicked. We had known each other a long time before now but that time something magical happened. We started dating and not long we started having real intimacy. For us, we were heading to the altar no matter how long. But along the line, everything broke apart. We had misunderstandings. And all hell broke loose. I was devastated. He had promise[d] he wouldn't leave. I wasn't myself. I had suicidal thoughts. I felt used and I was ashamed. Once, I came back from somewhere and I took all the drugs I could find in the house, wrote a letter to my mum. I was prepared to take them, I just wanted to be far away from the pain I was feeling. But something stopped me. I was so determined to give myself away that day. And today I'm thankful I didn't.

Q5. What helped you find freedom from sexual shame?

- Christ. I gave my life to him. I poured everything out to him, he saved me, took everything away including the shame I was walking around with. After my experience I was so empty, so depressed. Nobody knew but I was an emptyness shell inside. I was so down. No light in my life, no joy, no hope for tomorrow, no dreams, no goals. I was a living dead. But Christ came and took all of it away. He healed my poor and fragile heart. He healed my misery. He gave me hope and grace, one I wasn't worthy of. That is why till today my life is nothing without him.

Q6. What are specific things you've heard ministers say about sexuality that brought more shame than good?

- Well, Sex is a sin. That is true. Actually, I am very privileged to attend a church where condemning people rather than encouraging them to Christ is not often heard. But once in a while, during church service and the ministers talk about sexuality, you're sure to feel ashamed because you're a culprit. And you know it, deep down inside of you. You may even think you're being preached and the minister knows all you've done.

Q7. Please check off which of the following that you have struggled with.

- Pornography
- Masturbation

Appendix N

- Lust

Q8. Share how your family talked about sex in the home. Were they comfortable with it? Were you shamed for sexual thoughts, questions, or behaviors in the home?

- Down here in Nigeria in Africa where I am from. Sexuality is rarely discussed in homes. No one talks about it, but you're going to be threatened and warned never to bring home unwanted pregnancies. It's like this silent watchman that if noticed will bust everything open for everyone to hear. In my family specifically, I wasn't even the pep talk. I just knew that I was if I ever got pregnant I'd be thrown out of the house. That was it. I was never shamed, I mean nobody ever got to talk about it, so there's no place for shaming. Over here, out of 85 homes in 100, while growing up nobody cares [or] asks questions on sexuality or even dare[s] to showcase characteristics of it. My home is one of them. Although now I'm older, I'm free to talk about it, but I can't since I haven't been used to asking such questions.

Q9. Is there anything else you want to share about your story?

- I want to encourage everyone out there that is struggling with sexual shame. There is hope. As long as you're still alive, there is hope for you. Continue to struggle. Christ died so that we might be saved from our sins and that includes whatever is making us feel unworthy and dirty. Get Jesus, it may sound so unreal and too good to be true but once you get Jesus, he will take your sexual shame away. As the days will go by, you won't even remember them anymore. I am living a life above sin and sexual shame now. If I can do it, you can do it.

Appendix O
Zendaya (Participant #27)

Q1. Do I have your permission to use this survey in my research project and future books? Your name would be changed so that you would remain anonymous.

- Yes

Q2. In what year were you born? (Enter four-digit birth year; for example, 1976.)

- 1975

Q3. Are you a follower of Jesus Christ?

- Yes

Q4. Have you ever experienced sexual shame? Please share your story.

- Yes. Molested by my cousin when I was 11. My father who valued the appearance of women left us for a much younger woman when I was a pre-teen. I fell into a pattern of promiscuity in high school as a means of seeking love only to be greatly disappointed. I became a Christian in college and over time, assured of Christ's love for me and his atoning work on my behalf, I was washed clean and given new life. New life in Christ and a new life free from shame.

Appendix O

Q5. What helped you find freedom from sexual shame?

- Growing, over time, in my understanding of Christ's love for me.

Q6. What are specific things you've heard ministers say about sexuality that brought more shame than good?

- I can't think of anything

Q7. Please check off which of the following that you have struggled with.

- Promiscuity

Q8. Share how your family talked about sex in the home. Were they comfortable with it? Were you shamed for sexual thoughts, questions, or behaviors in the home?

- It was rarely talked about though my father had a pornography collection and commented on my appearance by telling me whether I was looking good or needed to lose weight.

Q9. Is there anything else you want to share about your story?

- I'm glad to be free!

Appendix P
Jennifer (Participant #35)

Q1. Do I have your permission to use this survey in my research project and future books? Your name would be changed so that you would remain anonymous.

- Yes

Q2. In what year were you born? (Enter four-digit birth year; for example, 1976.)

- 1984

Q3. Are you a follower of Jesus Christ?

- Yes

Q4. Have you ever experienced sexual shame? Please share your story.

- I was married for close to twenty years. He had an affair, and in retaliation I did too. Only I cheated with multiple people on serveral different occasions. It never stopped, until we ultimately divorced. I didn't experience too much shame from the outside, but on the inside, I was torn apart. I hated the things I had done, I felt worthless, unworthy. I was mortified at the thought of my children ever finding out. I wasn't sure how my new husband might feel about the things that had taken place in my past.

Appendix P

Q5. What helped you find freedom from sexual shame?

- At first allowing my husband to love me even while I knew he knew about my past, and he did that well. It was as if none of it mattered. Ultimately, it was realizing God[']s Grace in around May 2018. The Holy Spirit revealed to me that there was nothing I could do to be considered "good enough." That Jesus gave me His righteousness in exchange for my sin. And that I just needed to let God love me, I needed to receive His love. And when my eyes were opened to God[']s infinite, never ending love no matter the things I've done, He's waiting with open arms for me. My perspective was changed, I didn't allow the enemy to whisper into my ear any longer in an attempt to keep me down telling me I'd never be good enough.

Q6. What are specific things you've heard ministers say about sexuality that brought more shame than good?

- My daughter is lesbian, and she's experienced people telling her she'll go to hell if she doesn't change that. It's hard to be a believer and explain to her that being gay it's not Gods intended way but neither is any other type of sin that people indulge in or "believe" they are, that Christians like that, aren't a reflection of Jesus. That Jesus wouldn't be cruel in His intent to give you revelation of the sin you're walking in.

Q7. Please check off which of the following that you have struggled with.

- Lust
- Promiscuity

Q8. Share how your family talked about sex in the home. Were they comfortable with it? Were you shamed for sexual thoughts, questions, or behaviors in the home?

- Sex was spoken about freely. And in a fun nature or sometimes even crossed the line while telling stories of their experiences.

It was probably more encouraged without a healthy way of seeing sex or practicing.

Q9. Is there anything else you want to share about your story?

- It may be my own idea, but I think people who have been sexually violated as children tend to be promiscuous. Sometimes I've wondered if that[']s why I behaved the way I did.

Appendix Q
Aubrey (Participant #15)

Q1. Do I have your permission to use this survey in my research project and future books? Your name would be changed so that you would remain anonymous.

- Yes

Q2. In what year were you born? (Enter four-digit birth year; for example, 1976.)

- 1990

Q3. Are you a follower of Jesus Christ?

- Yes

Q4. Have you ever experienced sexual shame? Please share your story.

- Yes. A friend of a friend snuck something into my drink one night, and after just a drink or two, I couldn't remember a thing. After I was raped, I ran out of the apartment crying. on the drive home, my friend and I stopped at a gas station, and there was blood everywhere. I don't remember a lot about the night, other than I had to stop on the side of the road multiple times to throw up, but the sexual sin that followed, that I turned to men rather than turning to God was the worst. I became sexually active, and never felt good enough, no matter how many men I slept with. Only when I renewed my faith in Christ, and opened up about my past did I feel like I was enough.

Q5. What helped you find freedom from sexual shame?

- Turning to God, and finding a Christ centered community that could help me get over my shame and guilt has helped more than anything.

Q6. What are specific things you've heard ministers say about sexuality that brought more shame than good?

- I've opened up to my minister about my past, and he's been there. There was one time that I was trying to get out of the sexual past that I was prone to, and I was just having a terrible day, and wasn't feeling good enough, and I had a couple of drinks. My neighbor, who I was trying to teach about Jesus, took advantage of the situation. I told my minster about it, and although it had been about a year since I had had sex, and I had been doing well, I just had a moment where that sin took back over my life. My minister was rude about it, accusing me of doing it often and saying that if I do it again (even though it had been a year, and as if we all don't run back to our other sins daily), that I might need to stop coming to the church. Although it scared me into not doing it again (because I wasn't planning on it anyway), it has made me pull away from the church.

Q7. Please check off which of the following that you have struggled with.

- Masturbation
- Lust
- Promiscuity

Q8. Share how your family talked about sex in the home. Were they comfortable with it? Were you shamed for sexual thoughts, questions, or behaviors in the home?

Appendix Q

- My parents never talked about it. I told them about the rape, almost 4 years after it happened, and they never knew I had even had sex, even though I am 28 years old.

Q9. Is there anything else you want to share about your story?

- I just think that women should be more open to talking about what has happened to them, or what they are going through. I think the #MeToo movement has helped get women to talk about things, but we, as women, shouldn't shame other women just because we sin differently, or because we were in the wrong place at the wrong time. I think that we need to forgive as Christ forgave, and be there for people as He was. Thank you for being open about your story and giving women hope and faith in people in the spot light. Your story is incredible, and so are you! God Bless!

Appendix R
Stacy (Participant #28)

Q1. Do I have your permission to use this survey in my research project and future books? Your name would be changed so that you would remain anonymous.

- Yes

Q2. In what year were you born? (Enter four-digit birth year; for example, 1976.)

- 1993

Q3. Are you a follower of Jesus Christ?

- Yes

Q4. Have you ever experienced sexual shame? Please share your story.

- Growing up it was never safe to ask my parents (or anyone I knew) questions about sex. It would always turn into "I had done something wrong." I grew up feeling bad about my sexuality and soon turned to pornography and masturbation in secret because I couldn't open up to anyone about how I was struggling. I didn't know another woman who struggled with these things or even had sexual desire of her own. I thought I was the only one! Every book or sermon on the subject only mentioned male desire.

Appendix R

Q5. What helped you find freedom from sexual shame?

- It wasn't until a mentor led with vulnerability and shared about her own struggles that I felt safe to share my own sin. She pointed me to the gospel and how God knew the whole time and still sent Jesus to make a way for me to have relationship with him. This gave me the strength to keep being vulnerable with that mentor and pursue accountability and healing of those deeper issues. Over time I felt safe enough and secure in God to share my stories with others and help them start their recovery journey.

Q6. What are specific things you've heard ministers say about sexuality that brought more shame than good?

- "If you haven't experienced an orgasm, you haven't lived"—said during a sermon. "I'm sure the guys are talking about porn over there" said during a women's time that didn't address female porn uses. "I know women don't struggle with sex."

Q7. Please check off which of the following that you have struggled with.

- Pornography
- Masturbation
- Lust
- Promiscuity

Q8. Share how your family talked about sex in the home. Were they comfortable with it? Were you shamed for sexual thoughts, questions, or behaviors in the home?

- It was always bad. I got in trouble if I asked questions and so I stopped asking.

Q9. Is there anything else you want to share about your story?

- I have been in recovery for about five years now and I recently got married. We struggled sexually a lot before we got married and I knew marriage wouldn't fix me but I definitely thought it would help more. Six months in and I'm just not realizing how much I'm still an addict even though I have a "blessed" outlet for my sexual addiction. No one prepared me for how deep those underlying manipulations and need for control would be and how they would affect my spouse. Being in a group still that works through a recovery program has been so helpful to unmask some of those lies and wounds that I'm still experiencing as a married woman.

Appendix S
Brandi (Participant #11)

Q1. Do I have your permission to use this survey in my research project and future books? Your name would be changed so that you would remain anonymous.

- Yes

Q2. In what year were you born? (Enter four-digit birth year; for example, 1976.)

- 1987

Q3. Are you a follower of Jesus Christ?

- Yes

Q4. Have you ever experienced sexual shame? Please share your story.

- I stumbled onto dirty novels at my local library and eventually "graduated" to reading romance novels, erotica, and more! I also learned how to masturbate around this time and felt super guilty because I knew it wasn't God's best for me.

Q5. What helped you find freedom from sexual shame?

- Finding an accountability partner and confessing my sins. This helped me to repent and finally grab hold of the grace and forgiveness that Christ freely offers

Q6. What are specific things you've heard ministers say about sexuality that brought more shame than good?

- Although this never applied to me, I often heard pastors use negative examples to describe people who had sex before marriage. For example, describing people who have had sex outside of marriage as "used tissues, used cars," etc.

Q7. Please check off which of the following that you have struggled with.

- Masturbation
- Lust

Q8. Share how your family talked about sex in the home. Were they comfortable with it? Were you shamed for sexual thoughts, questions, or behaviors in the home?

- It wasn't discussed . . . at all. I learned about sex the way I learned about most things: reading online/books or talking to friends.

Q9. Is there anything else you want to share about your story?

- Nope

Appendix T
Carrie (Participant #44)

Q1. Do I have your permission to use this survey in my research project and future books? Your name would be changed so that you would remain anonymous.

- Yes

Q2. In what year were you born? (Enter four-digit birth year; for example, 1976.)

- 1985

Q3. Are you a follower of Jesus Christ?

- Yes

Q4. Have you ever experienced sexual shame? Please share your story.

- Exploring and struggling with pornography in college. A few times after college as well. Struggling with masturbation. Single for 10+ years after college and wondering if marriage will be in my future.

Q5. What helped you find freedom from sexual shame?

- In early college, my bible study leader shared (with permission) about her fiancé's struggle with porn to reach out to her group and offer someone to confide in and accountability partner if we were struggling in that or a similar area. I met with her and confessed my struggle which was relatively new. I am so thankful she took that step for our group and I was about to talk with her early on rather than dwelling in the struggle for a long period before trying to get help. She was already a safe person that I was connected to so it was a more comfortable opportunity to confess.

Q6. What are specific things you've heard ministers say about sexuality that brought more shame than good?

- There was often so much "do not's" that I think I missed healthy connections and friendships with the opposite sex.

Q7. Please check off which of the following that you have struggled with.

- Pornography
- Masturbation

Q8. Share how your family talked about sex in the home. Were they comfortable with it? Were you shamed for sexual thoughts, questions, or behaviors in the home?

- Very limited discussions other than a few specific talks or being given books to read at different ages. There was a focus on staying pure for marriage. The idea of discussing specific details with parents seemed way too awkward. I wouldn't view it as negative shame like it would have been terrible for me to ask questions but more awkwardness.

Q9. Is there anything else you want to share about your story?

- No, but thanks for what you are doing around this area to help people!

Appendix U
Jackie (Participant #38)

Q1. Do I have your permission to use this survey in my research project and future books? Your name would be changed so that you would remain anonymous.

- Yes

Q2. In what year were you born? (Enter four-digit birth year; for example, 1976.)

- 1994

Q3. Are you a follower of Jesus Christ?

- Yes

Q4. Have you ever experienced sexual shame? Please share your story.

- Yes, I struggled with a masturbation addiction, and I felt ashamed to confess it. There was a lack of healthy communication on sexuality between my mom and I.

Q5. What helped you find freedom from sexual shame?

- I first heard someone confess it, and it was evident they were freed and not defined by it. I felt free to share this with a church director when he mentioned he struggled with sexual brok[en]ness. Knowing there was a point of relating helped me not feel alone and was what I needed be vulnerable.

Q6. What are specific things you've heard ministers say about sexuality that brought more shame than good?

- The sexually immoral will not inherit the kingdom of God.

Q7. Please check off which of the following that you have struggled with.

- Masturbation

Q8. Share how your family talked about sex in the home. Were they comfortable with it? Were you shamed for sexual thoughts, questions, or behaviors in the home?

- My parents never addressed sex. My mom addressed me by telling me she could get me anti itch cream to keep me away from the private areas. I went with that idea bc I was too ashamed to admit there was something further than itching

Q9. Is there anything else you want to share about your story?

- Freedom is so good! I didn't seek help for years—until I was a young adult—bc I was nervous of the off chance it wasn't available to me. I wish so badly I went for freedom earlier. Whoever you are out there, you're not alone! I'm rooting for you, but most importantly God wants you freed. He doesn't want sin to entangle you bc he wants intimacy with you!

Appendix V
Juliana (Participant #24)

Q1. Do I have your permission to use this survey in my research project and future books? Your name would be changed so that you would remain anonymous.

- Yes

Q2. In what year were you born? (Enter 4-digit birth year; for example, 1976.)

- 1996

Q3. Are you a follower of Jesus Christ?

- Yes

Q4. Have you ever experienced sexual shame? Please share your story.

- I started struggling with masturbation in my early teens. For several years I was in denial of what I was doing, and for a few more I continued to make excuses for myself. I would push away my conviction about it so I would not have to address it. I was not open about this with anyone, even close Christian friends, until about 2 years ago. I think there is so much stigma around women and sexual sin and I felt that I would be judged or looked down upon if I shared.

Q5. What helped you find freedom from sexual shame?

- Over the past few years the Lord has convicted me more and more to the point where I cannot ignore it. Hearing other women's similar stories showed me that I was not alone and that my struggles with sexual sin do not disqualify me as a Christian. God has grown me so much—this may be a temptation I always have but He has granted me so much strength in fighting it and the conviction from the Holy Spirit I have is very effective at helping me to "flee from sexual immorality." And I am so thankful to know that I am not alone and I am not unloveable or unworthy. If I had not heard other womens' stories I may not have ever a) confronted my struggles head on or b) had the courage and the confidence in Christ to share my struggles—my sin does not own me and there is so much freedom in Christ.

Q6. What are specific things you've heard ministers say about sexuality that brought more shame than good?

- Respondent skipped this question.

Q7. Please check off which of the following that you have struggled with.

- Masturbation
- Lust

Q8. Share how your family talked about sex in the home. Were they comfortable with it? Were you shamed for sexual thoughts, questions, or behaviors in the home?

- I received a basic "talk" as a young child and then a more in-depth one at around age 12. Beyond that it was not a regular topic of conversation. I do not think the way my family discussed or didn't discuss sex had much impact, positive or negative, on the shame I would feel later on.

Q9. Is there anything else you want to share about your story?

- Respondent skipped this question.

Appendix W
Victoria (Participant #18)

Q1. Do I have your permission to use this survey in my research project and future books? Your name would be changed so that you would remain anonymous.

- Yes

Q2. In what year were you born? (Enter four-digit birth year; for example, 1976.)

- 1974

Q3. Are you a follower of Jesus Christ?

- Yes

Q4. Have you ever experienced sexual shame? Please share your story.

- Hello, I grew up in a physically, mentally and emotionally abusive household. This included a form of sexual harassment beginning around the age of 11-ish, Being called "Lard ass" (size 0 up to size 8), to statements such as "Oh, the neighbor boy really likes looking at your ass" to being called a whore and slut every day from 11-ish on. It was a vicious form of control and very degrading to my sense of self worth resulting in lifelong shame of my body anytime I became heavier than a size 10. (Today I am a size 16 and dislike it, but it provides me with "protection" from being looked at by men and being in any type of sexual relationship. My sexuality is either full blast and I date in very sex-focused relationships or completely off and do not date anyone. Currently I have been single for over 2 1/2 years after dating a man who attempted to rape me, then after breaking up with him, stalked me for a year before I changed my telephone number and moved. The police couldn't do anything because he did not actually rape me, nor did he hit me. Did this change my outlook? Heck yes! I now live a very peaceful life with my dog and NO dating. My life is filled with male and female platonic relationships and I continue to heal, grow closer to God, and mature. Sexual shame, to me, seems more outdated in our American culture and has eased up considerably since my youth.

Q5. What helped you find freedom from sexual shame?

- #1—Making the healthy choice to break off my relationship with my abusive father. He is no longer allowed in my life in any form. I wish him well, but have no energy for him. #2—Eight years of therapy ranging from cognitive behavior to EMDR. #3—Celebrate Recovery is AMAZING!! Listening to other women's stories and sharing the pain with others is remarkably healing. #4—God coming into my life. He shows us how to forgive and unconditional love.

Q6. What are specific things you've heard ministers say about sexuality that brought more shame than good?

- Any Catholic church service. Submission to men, disallowing birth control. No thank you.

Q7. Please check off which of the following that you have struggled with.

- Promiscuity

Appendix W

Q8. Share how your family talked about sex in the home. Were they comfortable with it? Were you shamed for sexual thoughts, questions, or behaviors in the home?

- Sex was something exciting to be bragged about among siblings, openly and inappropriately discussed about how my grandfather chased after his daughters when drunk attempting to rape them. Children should NOT hear these things and should be protected/kept away from their grandfather with this behavior. Again, my teen years included talking shamefully about my body changes in disrespectful ways. Any time I went out with female friends or on a date, I was called whore or slut. Always shame. Once I went out with my female friend and her boyfriend to a party. Well, I told my friend when we started drinking that I DID NOT want to sleep with or kiss the man hosting the party (he was too old—28ish and I was 16). I woke up the next morning naked next to him. I believe he drugged my drink and raped me, although I have no recollection. My parents found out this guy kissed me and teased me about "beer goggles." Why would they first, allow their daughter to stay out all night? and also, not mention the inappropriateness of kissing someone so much older?

Q9. Is there anything else you want to share about your story?

- Whew, that was very traumatic to write. I have worked so hard to right my life through therapy, positive, inspiring friends and support groups. We never fully "get over" the pain, but we can reshape our lives through God and friends.

Appendix X
Kayla (Participant #2)

Q1. Do I have your permission to use this survey in my research project and future books? Your name would be changed so that you would remain anonymous.

- Yes

Q2. In what year were you born? (Enter four-digit birth year; for example, 1976.)

- 1992

Q3. Are you a follower of Jesus Christ?

- Yes

Q4. Have you ever experienced sexual shame? Please share your story.

- A little. I grew up in a conservative household with a mother who was very embarrassed and jaded about all things sexual (and some romance) and a father who struggled with a pornography addiction. I remember being ashamed of my first crush (age 14/15) because I didn't want others to know that I had sexual desires (which are super normal and good of course). As I matured, I started to read books and blogs that made me realize how much God loves healthy, loving sex between a man and a woman who are married. I'm a single

Appendix X

woman who is learning how to be content in this season while also excited to one day (hopefully soon) begin a fun, passionate sex life with one man for life! :)

Q5. What helped you find freedom from sexual shame?

- Jesus Himself, the Bible (reading Song of Songs really helped), Christian sex blogs (that are healthy and Biblically based), talking to wise and mature female friends (many of them much older than I), and Christian books on God's high value of sex and sexuality as He intended it.

Q6. What are specific things you've heard ministers say about sexuality that brought more shame than good?

- That a person is defined by his or her sexual desires, that sex is the "end all, be all" of human life, and that sinning sexually is worse than other sins.

Q7. Please check off which of the following that you have struggled with.

- Respondent skipped this question.

Q8. Share how your family talked about sex in the home. Were they comfortable with it? Were you shamed for sexual thoughts, questions, or behaviors in the home?

- They weren't very comfortable with it—it was either not talked about or talked about in negative ways, often. I was shamed on occasion

Q9. Is there anything else you want to share about your story?

- Respondent skipped this question.

Appendix Y

Megan (Participant #42)

Q1. Do I have your permission to use this survey in my research project and future books? Your name would be changed so that you would remain anonymous.

- Yes

Q2. In what year were you born? (Enter four-digit birth year; for example, 1976.)

- 1998

Q3. Are you a follower of Jesus Christ?

- Yes

Q4. Have you ever experienced sexual shame? Please share your story.

- When I was eight years old, I was molested by my neighbor. I didn't know what happened that time, but when I grew older, I understood. It messed me up, I felt violated and unloved. Above all, I felt shame, and looking at myself today, I ask myself what if? Would I still be this way?

Q5. What helped you find freedom from sexual shame?

- I signed up for lots of programs [that were] helpful, even though it wasn't easy coming out of it . . .

Appendix Y

Q6. What are specific things you've heard ministers say about sexuality that brought more shame than good?

- That it's a sin. That you can't enjoy what God designed for you and your partner's enjoyment.

Q7. Please check off which of the following that you have struggled with.

- Pornography
- Masturbation
- Lust

Q8. Share how your family talked about sex in the home. Were they comfortable with it? Were you shamed for sexual thoughts, questions, or behaviors in the home?

- We never talked about sexuality in my home. All I know about sexuality is through movies and books. Have never been sat down and given the "talk" before.

Q9. Is there anything else you want to share about your story?

- Yes actually . . . sometimes I wonder how God could have allowed such to happen to me. When I was 18, I was raped again by a thief. This started me on a journey of self-loathing and selling myself short. Cause I believed I wasn't good enough. I believe I don't deserve the best cause [I] am damaged goods

Bibliography

Achour, Radhouane, et al. "Vaginismus and Pregnancy: Epidemiological Profile and Management Difficulties." *Psychology Research and Behavior Management* 12 (2019) 137-43. https://pubmed.ncbi.nlm.nih.gov/30881157/.

Adams, Kenneth M., and Donald W. Robinson. "Shame Reduction, Affect Regulation, and Sexual Boundary Development: Essential Building Blocks of Sexual Addiction Treatment." *Sexual Addiction and Compulsivity* 8.1 (2001) 23-44. https://www.tandfonline.com/doi/abs/10.1080/10720160127559.

Alexander, Calah. "Sloppy Seconds Sex Ed." *Patheos*, May 14, 2013. https://link.gale.com/apps/doc/EJ3010603221/OVIC?u=txshracd2698&sid=OVIC&xid=5ee8af1e.

Alix, Stéphanie, et al. "Self-Blame, Shame, Avoidance, and Suicidal Ideation in Sexually Abused Adolescent Girls: A Longitudinal Study." *Journal of Child Sexual Abuse* 29:4 (2019) 432-47. https://www.tandfonline.com/doi/abs/10.1080/10538712.2019.1678543?journalCode=wcsa20.

Allender, Dan B. *Healing the Wounded Heart: The Heartache of Sexual Abuse and the Hope of Transformation*. Grand Rapids: Baker, 2016.

Arata, Catalina M. "Coping with Rape: The Roles of Prior Sexual Abuse and Attributions of Blame." *Journal of Interpersonal Violence* 14 (1999) 62-78. https://doi.org/10.1177/088626099014001004.

Arens, Johannes. "Bound to Shame: Sexual Addiction and Christian Ethics." DThM diss., Durham University, 2011. http://etheses.dur.ac.uk/714/.

Birchard, Thaddeus. *CBT for Compulsive Sexual Behaviour: A Guide for Professionals*. London: Routledge, 2015.

Bluhm, Tiffany. *Prey Tell: Why We Silence Women Who Tell the Truth and How Everyone Can Speak Up*. Grand Rapids: Brazos, 2021.

Blum, Petra S. "Women, Sex, and God: Women's Sexuality and the Internalization of Religious Messages." PhD diss., University of Missouri, 2015. https://irl.umsl.edu/cgi/viewcontent.cgi?article=1135&context=dissertation.

Bolz-Weber, Nadia. *Shameless: A Sexual Reformation*. New York: Convergent, 2019.

Bibliography

Bridges, Jerry. *True Community*. Colorado Springs: NavPress, 2012.

Briere, John, et al. "Accumulated Childhood Trauma and Symptom Complexity." *Journal of Traumatic Stress* 21 (2008) 223–26. https://doi.org/10.1002/jts.20317.

Brown, Brené. *I Thought It Was Just Me (but It Isn't): Making the Journey from "What Will People Think?" to "I Am Enough."* New York: Avery, 2007.

———. "Listening to Shame." March 2012. TED video, 20:22. https://www.ted.com/talks/brene_brown_listening_to_shame.

———. "The Power of Vulnerability." June 2010. TED video, 20:03. https://www.ted.com/talks/brene_brown_on_vulnerability.

———. "Shame Resilience Theory: A Grounded Theory Study on Women and Shame." *Families in Society: The Journal of Contemporary Social Services* 87.1 (January 2006) 43–52. https://journals.sagepub.com/doi/10.1606/1044-3894.3483.

Brumberg, Joan Jacobs. *The Body Project: An Intimate History of American Girls*. New York: Vintage, 1998.

Carboneau, Ryan. "Religiosity, Moral Disapproval, Shame and Pornography Use: Assessing the Relationship Between Shame and Sexual Behaviors." PhD diss., Liberty University, 2018. https://digitalcommons.liberty.edu/cgi/viewcontent.cgi?article=2840&context=doctoral.

Carnes, Patrick. *Don't Call It Love: Recovery from Sexual Addiction*. New York: Bantam, 1991.

———. *Out of the Shadows: Understanding Sexual Addiction*. Center City, MN: Hazelden, 2001.

Chapin, Wendy Elizabeth. *Facing the Talk: Conversations with My Four Daughters about Sex*. Downers Grove, IL: InterVarsity, 2015.

Chisholm, Myles, and Terry Lynn Gall. "Shame and the X-Rated Addiction: The Role of Spirituality in Treating Male Pornography Addiction." *Sexual Addiction and Compulsivity* 22.4 (October 2, 2015) 259–72. https://www.tandfonline.com/doi/abs/10.1080/10720162.2015.1066279.

Cutrer, William, et al. *Sexual Intimacy in Marriage*. 4th ed. Grand Rapids: Kregel, 2020.

Dearing, Ronda L., et al. "On the Importance of Distinguishing Shame from Guilt: Relations to Problematic Alcohol and Drug Use." *Addictive Behaviors* 30.7 (August 1, 2005) 1392–1404. https://www.ncbi.nlm.nih.gov/pmc/articles/PMC3106346/.

DeMuth, Mary. *We Too: How the Church Can Respond Redemptively to the Sexual Abuse Crisis*. Eugene, OR: Harvest House, 2019.

Denton, Rudy A. "Utilising Forgiveness to Help Sexually Abused Adolescents Break Free from Guilt and Shame: A Pastoral Gestalt Theory." *Acta Theologica* 34.2 (2014) 5–28. https://www.ajol.info/index.php/actat/article/view/129815.

Dhuffar, Manpreet K., and Mark D. Griffiths. "Understanding the Role of Shame and Its Consequences in Female Hypersexual Behaviours: A Pilot

Bibliography

Study." *Journal of Behavioral Addictions* 3.4 (December 2014) 231–37. https://www.ncbi.nlm.nih.gov/pmc/articles/PMC4291828/.

Eckert, Kim Gaines. *Things Your Mother Never Told You: A Woman's Guide to Sexuality*. Downers Grove, IL: InterVarsity, 2014.

Farr, Corey. "A Single Man on Gender Roles and the Church." *Christianity Today*, December 27, 2019. https://www.christianitytoday.com/scot-mcknight/2019/december/single-man-on-gender-roles-and-church.html.

Feiring, Candice, et al. "Trying to Understand Why Horrible Things Happen: Attribution, Shame and Symptom Development Following Sexual Abuse." *Child Maltreatment* 7 (2002) 26–41. https://journals.sagepub.com/doi/10.1177/1077559502007001003.

Ferree, Marnie C. "Females and Sex Addiction: Myths and Diagnostic Implications." *Sexual Addiction and Compulsivity* 8 (2001) 287–300. https://www.tandfonline.com/doi/abs/10.1080/107201601753459973.

———., ed. *Making Advances: A Comprehensive Guide for Treating Female Sex and Love Addicts*. Royston, GA: Society for the Advancement of Sexual Health, 2012.

———. *No Stones: Women Redeemed from Sexual Shame*. Fairfax, VA: Xulon, 2002.

Frohwirth, Lori, et al. "Managing Religion and Morality within the Abortion Experience: Qualitative Interviews with Women Obtaining Abortions in the U.S." *World Med Health Policy* 10.4 (2018) 381–400. https://doi.org/10.1002/wmh3.289.

Fugère, Madeleine A., et al. "Sexual Attitudes and Double Standards: A Literature Review Focusing on Participant Gender and Ethnic Background." *Sexuality and Culture* 12 (2008) 169–82. https://doi.org/10.1007/s12119-008-9029-7.

Garcia, Lea A., "Pornography Use: The Lesser of Two Evils for Religious Emerging Adults." PhD diss., Liberty University, 2018. https://digitalcommons.liberty.edu/cgi/viewcontent.cgi?article=2832&context=doctoral.

Gervais, Sarah J., and M. Meghan Davidson. "Objectification among College Women in the Context of Intimate Partner Violence." In *Perspectives on College Sexual Assault: Perpetrator, Victim, and Bystander*, edited by Roland Maiuro, 83–96. New York: Springer, 2015.

Gilliland, Randy, et al. "The Roles of Shame and Guilt in Hypersexual Behavior." *Sexual Addiction and Compulsivity* 18.1 (2011) 12–29. https://www.tandfonline.com/doi/abs/10.1080/10720162.2011.551182.

Görg, Nora, et al. "Trauma-Related Emotions and Radical Acceptance in Dialectical Behavior Therapy for Posttraumatic Stress Disorder after Childhood Sexual Abuse." *Borderline Personality Disorder and Emotion Dysregulation* 2.1 (2017) 1–12. https://bpded.biomedcentral.com/articles/10.1186/s40479-017-0065-5.

Bibliography

Grant, Jonathan. *Divine Sex: A Compelling Vision for Christian Relationships in a Hypersexualized Age*. Grand Rapids: Brazos, 2015.

Gregoire, Sheila Wray, et al. *The Great Sex Rescue: The Lies You've Been Taught and How to Recover What God Intended*. Grand Rapids: Baker, 2021.

Grenz, Stanley. *Sexual Ethics: An Evangelical Perspective*. Louisville: Westminster John Knox, 1997.

Griffin, David A. "Shame Reduction in Sexually Addicted Men." DMin diss., Denver Seminary, 2007. https://rim.atla.com/node/32932.

Griffith, James, et al. "Pornography Actresses: An Assessment of the Damaged Goods Hypothesis." *Journal of Sex Research* 50.7 (November 2012) 1–12. https://www.tandfonline.com/doi/abs/10.1080/00224499.2012.719168.

Hastings, Anne Stirling. *Treating Sexual Shame: A New Map for Overcoming Dysfunction, Abuse, and Addiction*. Northvale, NJ: Jason Aronson, 1998.

The Healthy Colorado Youth Alliance. "Raising Expectations in the Rockies: Colorado's Abstinence-Only-until-Marriage Industry and the Imperative for Real Sex Education." September 9, 2010. SIECUS.org. https://siecus.org/wp-content/uploads/2018/07/Raising-Expectations-in-the-Rockies-Final-Posting.pdf.

Heath, Elaine. *Healing the Wounds of Sexual Abuse: Reading the Bible with Survivors*. Grand Rapids: Brazos, 2019.

Hirsch, Debra. *Redeeming Sex: Naked Conversations about Sexuality and Spirituality*. Downers Grove: InterVarsity, 2015.

Holcomb, Justin S., and Lindsey A. Holcomb. *Rid of My Disgrace: Hope and Healing for Victims of Sexual Assault*. Wheaton, IL: Crossway, 2011.

Hottenstein, Joy L. "Femininity, Masculinity, Gender, and the Role of Shame on Christian Men and Women in the Evangelical Church Culture." PsyD diss., George Fox University, 2014. https://digitalcommons.georgefox.edu/cgi/viewcontent.cgi?article=1157&context=psyd&httpsredir=1&referer=.

Humbert, Cynthia. *Deceived by Shame, Desired by God*. Colorado Springs: NavPress, 2001.

Jones, Beth Felker. *Faithful: A Theology of Sex*. Grand Rapids: Zondervan, 2015.

Kemish, Karen. "Psychological Distress in Adult Survivors of Childhood Sexual Abuse: The Role of Shame, Self-Esteem and Blame." DClinPsy diss., Bangor University, 2007. https://research.bangor.ac.uk/portal/files/20571423/null.

Klein, Linda Kay. *Pure: Inside the Evangelical Movement that Shamed a Generation of Young Women and How I Broke Free*. New York: Touchstone, 2018.

Kyle, Sarah E. "Identification and Treatment of Sexual Shame: Development of a Measure Tool and Group Therapy Protocol." PhD diss., American Academy of Clinical Sexologists, 2013. http://www.esextherapy.com/dissertations/Sarah%20E%20Kyle%20Identification%20and%20Treatment%20of%20Sexual%20Shame%20Development%20of%20a%20Measurement%20Tool%20and%20Group%20Therapy%20Protocol.pdf.

Bibliography

Langberg, Diane. *Suffering and the Heart of God: How Trauma Destroys and Christ Restores*. Greensboro, NC: New Growth, 2015.

May, Gerald G. *Addiction and Grace: Love and Spirituality in the Healing of Addictions*. San Francisco: HarperOne, 2006.

McClintock, Karen. *Sexual Shame: An Urgent Call to Healing*. Minneapolis: Augsburg Fortress, 2001.

———. *Shame-Less Lives, Grace-Full Congregations*. Herndon, VA: Alban Institute, 2012.

McDowell, Josh. *The Porn Phenomenon: The Impact of Pornography in the Digital Age*. Ventura, CA: Barna Group, 2016.

Murray, Kelly M., et al. "Spirituality, Religiosity, Shame and Guilt as Predictors of Sexual Attitudes and Experiences." *Journal of Psychology and Theology* 35.3 (2007) 222–34. https://doi.org/10.1177/009164710703500305.

Neill, Vicki. "Problematic Sexual Beliefs and Behaviors in the Church: A Content Analysis of Faith-Based Curricula Related to Evidence-Based Interventions." PhD diss., Liberty University, 2018. https://digitalcommons.liberty.edu/cgi/viewcontent.cgi?article=2852&context=doctoral.

Nelson, Heather Davis. *Unashamed: Healing Our Brokenness and Finding Freedom from Shame*. Wheaton, IL: Crossway, 2016.

Pattison, Stephen. *Shame: Theory, Therapy, Theology*. Cambridge: Cambridge University Press, 2000.

Paul, John, II. *Man and Woman He Created Them: A Theology of the Body*. Translated by Michael Waldstein. Boston: Pauline, 2006.

Perry, Samuel. *Addicted to Lust: Pornography in the Lives of Conservative Protestants*. New York: Oxford University Press, 2019.

"Pornhub's 2021 Year in Review: The Searches That Defined the Year with Aria." December 15, 2021. Video, 10:00. https://www.youtube.com/watch?v=AjI44z8mL38.

Prosek, Elizabeth A., et al. "Experiencing Shame: Collegiate Alcohol Abuse, Religiosity, and Spirituality." *Journal of College Counseling* 20.2 (July 2017) 126–38. https://onlinelibrary.wiley.com/doi/10.1002/jocc.12065.

Reavey, Paula, and Brendan Gough. "Dis/Locating Blame: Survivors' Constructions of Self and Sexual Abuse." *Sexualities* 3.3 (2000) 325–46. https://journals.sagepub.com/doi/10.1177/136346000003003003.

Rhea, Rob, and Klaus Issler. "Understanding the Relationship of Identity Status, Agency, and Religiosity on the Acceptance and Use of Pornography in Christian, Undergraduate Emerging Adults." *Journal of Psychology and Christianity* 34.2 (2015) 155–67. link.gale.com/apps/doc/A426900892/AONE?u=anon~cfceb2b2&sid=googleScholar&xid=944b1383.

Rinehart, Paula. *Sex and the Soul of a Woman: How God Restores the Beauty of Relationship from the Pain of Regret*. Grand Rapids: Zondervan, 2004.

Roberts, Matthias. *Beyond Shame: Creating a Healthy Sex Life on Your Own Terms*. Minneapolis: Fortress, 2020.

Bibliography

Rough, Bonnie J. *Beyond Birds and Bees: Bringing Home a New Message to Our Kids about Sex, Love, and Equality.* New York: Seal, 2018.

Rutledge, Fleming. *The Crucifixion: Understanding the Death of Jesus Christ.* Grand Rapids: Eerdmans, 2015.

Schaumburg, Harry W. *False Intimacy: Understanding the Struggle of Sexual Addiction.* Colorado Springs: NavPress, 1992.

Sellers, Tina Schermer. *Sex, God, and the Conservative Church.* New York: Routledge, 2017.

Skarka, Joy Pedrow. "Forced Sexuality: Rape." In *Sanctified Sexuality: Valuing Sex in an Oversexed World*, edited by Sandra L. Glahn and C. Gary Barnes, 273–89. Grand Rapids: Kregel, 2020.

Slattery, Juli. *Rethinking Sexuality: God's Design and Why It Matters.* Colorado Springs: Multnomah, 2018.

Stockitt, Robin. *Restoring the Shamed: Towards a Theology of Shame.* Eugene, OR: Cascade, 2012.

Stringer, Jay. *Unwanted: How Sexual Brokenness Reveals Our Way to Healing.* Carol Stream, IL: NavPress, 2018.

Struthers, William. *Wired for Intimacy: How Pornography Hijacks the Male Brain.* Downers Grove, IL: InterVarsity, 2009.

Szymanski, Dawn M. "Sexual Objectification, Internalization, and College Women's Depression: The Role of Shame." *The Counseling Psychologist* 48.1 (2019) 135–56. https://doi.org/10.1177/0011000019878847.

Thompson, Curt. *The Soul of Shame: Retelling the Stories We Believe about Ourselves.* Downers Grove, IL: InterVarsity, 2015.

Van der Kolk, Bessel A. *The Body Keeps the Score: Brain, Mind, and Body in the Healing of Trauma.* New York: Penguin, 2015.

Volk, Fred, et al. "Religiosity, Developmental Context, and Sexual Shame in Pornography Users: A Serial Mediation Model." *Sexual Addiction and Compulsivity* 23.2–3 (April 2, 2016) 244–59. https://www.tandfonline.com/doi/full/10.1080/10720162.2016.1151391.

Wade, Lisa D., et al. "The Incidental Orgasm: The Presence of Clitoral Knowledge and the Absence of Orgasm for Women." *Women Health* 42.1 (2005) 117–38. https://pubmed.ncbi.nlm.nih.gov/16418125/.

Watkins, Christine. *Do Abstinence Programs Work?* New York: Greenhaven, 2014.

Weiss, Karen G. "Too Ashamed to Report: Deconstructing the Shame of Sexual Victimization." *Feminist Criminology* 5.3 (2010) 286–310. https://journals.sagepub.com/doi/10.1177/1557085110376343.

West, Christopher. *Our Bodies Tell God's Story: Discovering the Divine Plan for Love, Sex, and Gender.* Grand Rapids: Brazos, 2020.

———. *Theology of the Body for Beginners.* West Chester, PA: Ascension, 2004.

Wilson, Marie. "Creativity and Shame Reduction in Sex Addiction Treatment." *Sexual Addiction and Compulsivity* 7.4 (December 2000) 229–48. https://www.tandfonline.com/doi/abs/10.1080/10720160008403699.

Bibliography

Winner, Lauren F. *Real Sex: The Naked Truth about Chastity*. Grand Rapids: Brazos, 2011.

Yuan, Christopher. *Holy Sexuality and the Gospel: Sex, Desire, and Relationships Shaped by God's Grand Story*. Colorado Springs: Multnomah, 2018.

www.ingramcontent.com/pod-product-compliance
Lightning Source LLC
Chambersburg PA
CBHW062043220426
43662CB00010B/1626